What People say about *The Nonviolent Communicatio*

In April – May 2010 we had the w̶ ̶ ̶ ̶ ̶ ̶ ̶ ̶ ̶ ̶ ̶ ̶ ̶ ̶ .. our society. Once again, my colleagues and I used mediation skills in acting as the third party in conflict. In one incident, a friend and I were in the middle of a conflict between a group of anti-government protesters and a group of soldiers who were holding rifles in postures ready to shoot. We ran between the two sides and helped them communicate with each other. Finally, the problem was solved peacefully and no one was injured. I used mediation skills at my best efforts to save not only other people's lives but also my own.

At the personal level, the mediation skills I learned from Liv and Kay[1] helped ground me when facing violent conflicts. I used these skills when dealing with people from all sides, who were full of anger, fear, and grief. Seeing how mediation skills learned from Liv and Kay worked in the midst of conflicts and could save lives, I would recommend them to anyone.

- Pairin Jotisakulratana Peace activist Thailand

I appreciate the attention to the underlying thinking that exacerbates conflict and also the shift of consciousness that invites conflict as a way of deepening our understanding and connection.

- Jori Manske, Restorative Mediator and CNVC certified trainer

I have grown to have a deep appreciation for Liv's incorporation of Nonviolent Communication into her life. When I heard that she had written a book on what she has learned in offering trainings in NVC mediation, I was pleased because of my personal dream of trainers offering NVC mediation trainings . I am confident that Liv's book will lead the way for trainers and mediators in many places."

- Ike Lasater, author of Words That Work In Business: A Practical Guide to Effective Communication in the Workplace

---

1   Mediation colleague

I thoroughly enjoy Liv and Kay's mediation training. They have broken down an art form into specific, do-able steps that I can follow and practice. I particularly like their easy-to-remember "hand" skill map where each finger represents a mediation skill. First, we work with a skill through written exercises so we have some time to think about it. Then, we try out each skill in a mediation triad format, and progress to combining them together into more complex skills. So, from something I find daunting and difficult, Liv and Kay have turned mediation into a fun, fast pace learning experience. My deep appreciation to both of you!!

- Kanya Peaceworker and NVC teacher in Thailand

This book is like a GPS system that helps you navigate through the process of learning mediation with ease, no matter if you are a single parent whose kids are fighting every day or a professional relationship counselor. With each practical exercise you complete, you will gain confidence in your mediation skills. You will find out where your strengths and growing edges in mediation are, and thus be able to practice more efficiently. The self-reflection exercises will invite you to deeply inquire into your motivation for mediating, allowing you to be aware where e.g. your passion for people's freedom of choice might turn into a blind spot. With the toolbox that this book provides, rather than hoping that you would know what to do when others are fighting and when so many things are happening at the same time, you will have clear focal points for your attention.

I used to think of mediation as something that only people with years of professional training and experience could do and to feel overwhelmed when others started fighting. Nowadays I lead workshops that help advanced NVC practitioners refine their mediation skills. "The helping hand" has been a major instrument in turning me from a cheering observer of Marshall Rosenberg's international mediation successes into someone passionately teaching and mentoring others.

- Ariane Korth, Undefend Yourself Trainer,
BayNVC Leadership Program '10 Participant and '11 Assistant Trainer

A Helping Hand

Mediation with
Nonviolent Communication
2nd Edition

Liv Larsson

Friare Liv Konsult
Mjösjölidvägen 477,946 40 Svensbyn
Sweden
Info @friareliv.se
www.friareliv.se

If you have not purchased this book directly from us, e-mail or call us if you wish to receive our book catalogue and newsletter.

Friare Liv AB
Mjösjölidvägen 477
946 40 Svensbyn
Sweden
Phone: + 46 911 24 11 44
info@friareliv.se
www.friareliv.se/eng

Author: Liv Larsson
Translation: Johan Rinman
Layout: Kay Rung
Cover design: Vilhelm PH Nilsson www.communicationforlife.org/vilhelm/

ISBN 978-91-976672-7-2

Contents

Preface

I grew up in Norrbotten, in northern Sweden, and it was common to be either directly or distantly related to the people one met. On numerous occasions while growing up, I was both irritated and felt embarrassed when my parents would start every new acquaintance trying to figure out how we were related to each other.

When I started to get interested in conflict resolution and mediation, I realized that there were actually reasons to appreciate this interest in kinship. I was helped by seeing that this exploration can contribute in a constructive way to conflict resolution, by making it clear that we are connected, and how our actions can affect others. I realized that there are certain cultures, for example in New Guinea, that deal with conflicts by having a third party help the people involved better understand how they are related to each other. In this way it becomes clear how their own actions can affect both their closest family and relatives, and even target themselves.

One of the principles in Nonviolent Communication (NVC), the approach that this book draws upon, is that we are interdependent. The purpose of NVC is to create a connection between us where we wish for everyone's needs to be considered and met to the greatest possible extent. To be able to create this quality of connection, we have to be willing to realize that our actions affect others.

Many of us act as a third party daily, though we might not think of ourselves as mediators. This can be in situations where we actively try to understand, and maybe intervene, when it seems others are struggling to connect. This can be between children, people in our workgroup, or among friends.

The founder of NVC, Marshall Rosenberg, has mediated in different conflict situations around the world for over 40 years. Rosenberg views needs as the common driving force behind everything humans do. He understands all emotional experiences to be dependent upon whether our needs are being met or not, and his discoveries have been of great help for me in my work as a mediator. There are many approaches to mediation. I have chosen to deepen my understanding of NVC because it contains very concrete tools that have strengthened my ability to act as a third party.

"Genuine cooperation is inspired when participants trust that their own needs and values will be respectfully addressed. The Nonviolent Communication process is based on respectful practices that foster genuine cooperation."

Marshall Rosenberg[1]

When I first started to mediate, it was a big challenge for me. However, I gradually learned how different parts of NVC could be woven together as a whole. This helped me to develop my mediation skills and became the foundation for the exercises in this book. I have worked things out over a period of many years and I hope that what I share can facilitate your ability to act as a third party in an effective way. With this taken into consideration, I have also written a chapter with exercises to inspire you in actively practicing mediation.

Summary

The book begins with an overview of mediation (chapters 1-2). Concepts about human nature, and views about conflict and justice are discussed here. Chapters 3 and 4 contain reflections on passivity, revenge, forgiveness, shame and guilt. Thereafter follows two chapters about how Nonviolent Communication can be used in mediation (chapters 5 and 6). In order to mediate, most of us need to practice, therefore chapter 7 contains exercises that give you access to various tools that you can use during mediation. Chapter 8 deals with the preparation for, and carrying out of, formal mediation.

The style of mediation that this book is mainly focusing on is a very direct mediation style. In some settings and some cultures this style might be perceived as too direct. In chapter 9, I present some other variations of mediation that I hope will be helpful in these situations. I also mention the concepts of "mediation in crime" and "restorative justice".

In chapter 10, mediation between children is illustrated. Throughout the book I have chosen to designate the parties as person A and person B or party A and B in the presented narratives. My hope is that this will

---

1. Rosenberg, Marshall (2008), We can work it out. Puddle Dancer Press.

contribute to the ease of the readers, both in following the theoretical discussions and in doing the exercises that I suggest. Mediation sometimes involves mediating between more than two people or two groups. The exercises in the book can be changed to fit these situations.

I use examples from my own experiences, as well as some from the experiences of others. To protect these people or groups, some changes have been made regarding personal information and places.

Good luck!

Chapter 1

Mediation

What is mediation?

Conflict always contains gifts. Mediation can be seen as an opportunity to open a present that until now has been wrapped up, and as a result to be able to finally appreciate the gift inside. A mediator or third party can be the one who does the opening, in the case the gift (the conflict) has come in a very challenging wrapping.

Mediation is a process where someone helps others to change their views about a conflict, to look beyond it, to see its potential for development and, together with the other parties, to reach agreement about how they want to relate in the future.

One of the things a mediator can do in handling a conflict is to help all involved gain a more humane view of each other. When we see each other's humanity we recognize ourselves, and our compassion awakes. This also creates more ease around the process of working towards enabling everyone to have their needs met.

The principles upon which I base this book are the same which underlie Nonviolent Communication (NVC). These principles can be used during mediation to help people find solutions to a specific problem. The same principles can also be used when people want reconciliation around something that has happened where mutual trust is difficult to experience.

In its most simple form, mediation is facilitating a conversation. As a mediator, you help the parties to communicate in a way that leads to understanding and connection between them, instead of continuing to communicate in ways that lead to resistance and confrontation.

A common motive for mediation is to heal relationships that are being experienced as painful, where people are struggling with mutual trust. Mediation is especially valuable when we have tough-to-solve conflicts in relationships that we really care about (for example with family members, friends, neighbors or colleagues).

In Sweden, and in many places around the world, mediation related to crime has proven to be a valuable opportunity in healing painful experiences.

When you use NVC to mediate, you focus primarily on creating connection between all parties. This connection is fundamental in finding solutions where everyone's needs are cared for and met to the greatest possible extent. No matter what has previously happened, as a mediator you focus on connection.

The special kind of connection that I am talking about is built on mutual respect and freedom of choice amongst all parties involved. Sometimes you don't reach solutions that work for everyone, but when the parties see each other's humanity, the trust that it is possible to connect deepens. This leads to greater creativity in finding new solutions and strategies. You have taken important steps towards reconciliation if after a meditation the parties have greater trust between them, feel hopeful and have gained a deeper connection. If they also have received new tools enabling them to heal their relationship, you are well on the way to helping them find a solution where everyone's needs are considered.

Our view of human nature affects our ability to mediate

When you start to practice mediation it can feel overwhelming and difficult. I believe that everyone can mediate, but that it requires a lot of practice to be able to do it in a way that satisfies you. The most important thing to be clear about as a mediator is your view of human nature and life in general. When you have a view of human nature that believes in the potential for reconciliation, I trust that you will easily be able to use the mediation tools to act as a third party in a natural way.

Our view of human nature is shaped by the society we grow up in and by the role models we have in that society. In her book *"The Chalice and the Blade, Our History, Our Future"*, the cultural historian Riane Eisler describes the battle that has lasted for thousands of years between what she calls the "Partnership Model" and the "Domination Model".[1] Both she and theologian Walter Wink[2] make clear in their writings how, during the last 10,000 years[3] societies have been created almost everywhere in the world that are structured according to the "Domination Model".

In his book "The Powers That Be," Wink describes how organizations

1   Eisler, Riane (2005), The Chalice and the Blade, our History, our Future. Eisler uses the term Partnership culture to describe a more life-serving system.
2   Wink, Walter (2000), The Powers That Be. Theology for a New Millennium. Doubleday Image.
3   I feel hopeful when I think about this as from a human perspective, 10, 000 years is not a very long time.

based on domination have hierarchical power structures as well as possess an inequitable distribution of resources and privileges. Coercion, violence or ranking of some kind is frequently used to maintain order. These are structures where a few dominate the many in maintaining control and order. Many of our families, schools, associations, religious congregations, businesses and governments continue to be governed in this way.

In systems based on domination, the view of human beings is, at its essence, that people are basically selfish and violent. If we assume that this is our true nature, then it follows that people need to be controlled or kept in check so that no one will come to harm.

Since we in that system have learned to compare and rank, there are many of us who believe that some people are a little better (or at least less bad) than others. The people who are "good" are given the right to govern and lead the others. In order to determine who will govern, there has been, throughout the past millennia, a constant struggle about who is "good" and who is "bad". Those who have reached the top in this kind of system will try to control people by using their power over them; first and foremost by means of punishment and reward.

Those who submit to doing what the authorities want them to do are rewarded and those who do not submit are punished. With the perception that people are selfish and violent, punishment and reward seem to be the most effective way to teach people how to behave. The idea is that punishment (or the deprivation of reward) will show us how bad we are and how we have done something wrong. In similar ways, we understand that we are approved of since those in power (parents, teachers, executives etc.) confirm it by rewarding us in some way. We learn that our value as humans lies in whether we are approved of by the authorities or not. This view of human beings functions as a justification for those who are in a position of superiority to have the right to dominate and control others, because that is how we humans learn about what is right and wrong. This is what is important to learn in order to live in a culture based on ranking and domination.

This view of human beings also includes the idea that when a conflict occurs, there must be someone who is guilty, a "bad guy". The impact of this idea has created extremely resourceful and effective ways of finding and prosecuting the "bad guys". Most of us are incredibly well trained in this way of thinking; in comparing and judging what is good and what is bad. Just reflect upon your own thoughts during the time you have read the last paragraph. How many times have you judged the system I describe as bad, wrong or unjust? Or, you may have judged my thoughts as wrong, "airy-fairy" or unrealistic. Given our huge amount of indoctrination in this way of thinking about right and wrong, it is not strange to find that we think in this way most of the time.

When I see (in my opinion) the lethal combination of high technology and domination thinking that seems to govern large parts of the world right now, I can easily lose hope. I believe we need to move away from seeing the world from the domination "myth" perspective, which is currently having enormously tragic effects on our planet, and move towards seeing the world in a way that better promotes life.

A need-based view of human nature

Focusing on the following two assumptions, which NVC is based upon, makes me more hopeful and inspires me to keep trying to mediate:

- **Everything we humans do, we do in order to try to satisfy our needs.**
- **As humans we want to contribute to each other if it is done without coercion.**

These assumptions help me remember that what I describe as a domination system is a choice about how to relate to the world. The two assumptions above are also choices, and very unlike the way of seeing the world many of us have been taught to see. However, we are always free to choose how we view each other and the world.

I want to make it clear that I see the idea of violence as redemptive as a myth. It is only one way to try to find a solution to problems, and we can replace it with an entirely different one.

When we make the choice to focus on what people need, instead of who has done right or who has done wrong, I think we significantly increase our chances of creating a world where there is space for everyone. This approach towards people is also helpful for the one who takes on the role of mediator, because it makes it easier to see the humanness in each person, regardless of how that person may have acted. This attitude and view of human beings permeates this book and is the basis for the practical exercises.

The idea that conflicts occur because there are needs that are not satisfied, gives me confidence that we could create a world that looks completely different than the one we live in today. What if the same amount of resources now used for weapons, military, police and prisons, would instead be spent on repairing relationships and learning new strategies that take everyone's needs into account. In that world there would probably automatically be a recognized place for mediators.

Mediation as a natural part of our culture?

I would like to answer this question based on the two different ways of thinking outlined in the paragraph above. One answer is based on a system of control and domination; the other based on a system with the purpose of serving life and meeting needs.

In a system based on domination, mediation is very rarely seen as a natural method of dealing with conflict, because conflicts are seen as something bad and are, at best, to be avoided. Violence or the threat of violence is instead the typical way of handling conflicts that occur in this system. One can also deal with conflicts by trying to avoid them all together with the help of control and a substantiated threat to resort to violence, if a conflict arises. These actions are performed or sanctioned by those in power, to restore order if it is disrupted. In a system based on domination there is great confidence in the enforcement of peace through control and violence. This is because after violence comes harmony, right...?

I would say that it is this way of thinking that creates and preserves the myth that violence is both necessary and has the potential of leading to harmony. It is this myth that domination cultures are based on and which evaluates violence as a strategy for solving conflicts. It makes violence and revenge or retaliation seem natural. Moreover, it preserves the imbalance of power which consists of a few people having power *over* the large majority.

In systems based on domination one seeks for someone to blame for having created a conflict. One finds the guilty one(s), decides what punishment seems "fair" and then punishes the person (or group). This way of dealing with conflict is based upon the belief that people learn new behaviors best when they hate or feel really bad about themselves; when they feel guilt, shame or fear of punishment. This is a tragic way of creating change, since it seldom leads to reconciliation or cooperation. Many times it leads instead to more violence in the form of revenge. And if revenge is not appealing, violence can instead be turned inward, which can lead to depression and bitterness.

It is not possible to decide what kind of culture we are dealing with by determining if conflicts arise or not. The difference lies in the way one views conflicts and how one deals with them.

If the cultural norm says that conflict is a sign of abnormality or of somebody having done something wrong, we will hesitate to admit that we could benefit from mediation. This is because if we admit that we have a conflict, we admit that we are not perfect. In cultures that view conflicts as something natural that can be learned from, there is instead an interest in spending time and energy working with the conflicts. When conflicts arise in life-serving systems, they are dealt with by trying to understand what they are about, instead of trying to smother them or fight them. Mediation becomes a way to learn as much as possible from the conflict.

Some cultures have social structures where the role of the "third party" is a built-in part of their system. They have seen the value of dealing with conflicts in that way and doing so at an early stage. Examples of this can be found among the native Indian tribes of North and South America, among the Maori people in New Zeeland, and groups on New Guinea and in Southeast Asia.

When our culture promotes a view of human nature that is based upon the notion that people do what they do in order to meet needs, and that humans want to contribute to others if they can do so freely, then mediation will be a natural part of our society and culture.

A mediation talk will then not be a separate event but will be seen as a part of a process in which all parts are important in the restorative process.

Justice has to be done???

One of the obstacles you may encounter when trying to mediate is the view that a conflict stems from someone doing something wrong, and that justice must be administered. This means that someone be punished, in order to put things right. If we do not find the guilty person, we want to find a scapegoat that can be sacrificed, as we long for harmony and for things to go back to normal. The intention is good, but we often miss the target.

It is easy to miss the fact that there is something in the system itself that leads to conflicts. We mistakenly think that the main problem is that a person should have behaved differently. Since we are fully occupied with finding and punishing the "Guilty", we fail to try to change the system itself that contributes to the conflict.

When we have learned that justice means giving someone what he or she *deserves*, conflict resolution runs the risk of only being a fight about who will be rewarded and who will be punished. This attitude permeates most of our legal system, most grade-and payment systems, as well as many other systems of control, reward and punishment.

When a mediator uses NVC, focus is on creating connection between the parties in order to then find a way to satisfy everyone's needs. The idea of who the guilty party is or what is "fair", is counterproductive because what we as members of a domination culture call justice is then more of an euphemism for revenge.

If the parties in a conflict do not trust that everyone's needs will be taken into account, the concept of "deserve" will often be used as a handrail. Mediation strives to create the trust that everyone's needs will be cared for to the greatest extent possible. It is then easier to drop the idea that someone must be punished for what has happened. In this mode, it becomes clear that behind the quest for justice there is a strong wish to have one's needs met. What becomes essential is figuring out what the parties can do to repair what is broken, whether in tangible things, relationships or trust.

Our words carry our view of human nature

"...it started long ago with myths about human nature that framed humans as basically evil and selfish - and that the good life is heroic forces crushing evil forces. We have been living under this destructive mythology for a long time, and it comes complete with a language that dehumanizes people and turns them into objectives."
Marshall Rosenberg[1]

An additional challenge to being a third party in a culture based on domination is the language. Most of us have learned to use an enormous amount of words to describe what people are. This means that we easily analyze each other, to assess what is normal or abnormal, appropriate or inappropriate, good or bad. NVC can be very helpful in that we receive concrete tools to translate all static expressions into a language that makes people more human. NVC uses a process language based on what we do and what we *need*, instead of a static language based on what we think someone *is*.

There are other ways to look at the world besides believing that order is maintained and created through systems of control and punishment. NVC is based on the idea that we humans enjoy contributing to each other when we feel it is voluntary, and when we understand how our actions affect others. This approach is neither based on the idea that people are good nor on the idea that they are evil, rather that we humans are acting to try to satisfy our needs. To support this view of human beings, we need to learn to communicate from the heart, instead of from a rule-driven world governed by right and wrong thinking where we blindly obey authorities. We need a language that can help us to clarify the life-serving intention that is disguised in a language based on domination and control.

I believe everyone has the ability to mediate, but we need to receive practical tools for getting in touch with the needs people are trying to satisfy in all situations of life. You need to transform your theoretical understanding of how mediation works into a language that creates connection and inspires compassion. Therefore, apart from theory, this book also contains concrete exercises that you will hopefully find of great advantage in training your ability to act as a third party.

---

1 Rosenberg, Marshall (2005), Speak Peace In A World Of Conflict, What You Say Next Will Change Your World. Puddle Dancer Press.

Chapter 2

The dream
- a world without
conflict?

Conflict – crisis or possibility?

Conflicts can be described in this way:

A conflict is an interaction between at least two parties where at least one party
1) has desires that are felt to be too important to be given up, and
2) perceives that the other party is obstructing the fulfillment of those desires.
Thomas Jordan[1]

If you want to contribute to solving conflicts, there are a couple of things you need to be clear about. This can help you to see when and how you can act in dealing with the conflict.

One thing to watch out for is when someone makes evaluations, uses labels and/or makes an analysis about what has happened. We must actually separate these from that which has happened. Be also conscious about if someone involved in the conflict starts looking for who is right and who is wrong. When someone does this there is a great risk of taking sides. The conflict may get stuck and becomes more difficult to handle.

If you notice that this is happening, focus your attention on the needs that are not being met. To focus on needs (both on our own and other's) often creates more connection between people than if the people involved are trying to find scapegoats, focusing on who has done wrong and who should behave differently. When the people involved in the conflict know what they need, it becomes easier to find strategies that are satisfying for all parties.

Our view of conflicts affects how we deal with them. I see conflicts as perishable and, like fresh produce, after a short period of time they start to go bad. We often wait to deal with conflicts in the hope that they will diminish or disappear. However, it is seldom easier to handle a conflict just by waiting. The solution is only delayed.

Because so many of us have learned that conflict signals that something is wrong, it is not strange that we shy away from trying to deal with them. We end up letting them get even bigger. My hope is that you, with the

1 Jordan, Thomas (2007), Att hantera och förebygga konflikter på arbetsplatsen. Lärarforbundet.

help of this book, will start to act, to mediate conflict earlier and to do so in a way that leads to connection and cooperation.

Moreover, I view conflict as a valuable element in all human relationships. Conflicts help us grow as individuals and as societies. When it becomes a societal or judicial system's responsibility to take care of conflicts we risk missing an opportunity to experience how we are interconnected. If we instead ask ourselves how the conflict affects each and every one of us, there is a chance of making a change that will benefit everyone. For me, mediation is about letting people have conflicts in ways that are peaceful and that we can learn from.

Summary of how to handle conflicts

1. Get all the cards on the table (things that can clarify the situation).

2. See everyone involved as fellow human beings (understand feelings, needs, dreams).

3. Get clear about what all parties want to happen (requests).

After having mediated in hundreds of conflicts, I have great trust that human relationships can be restored, even if it is sometimes a great challenge (and sometimes takes more time and energy than we really want to spend).

Handling conflict - Two different views

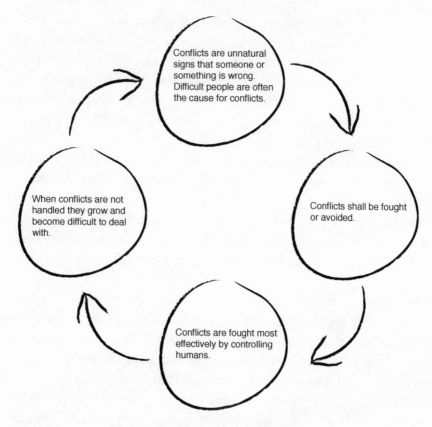

Conflicts are unnatural signs that someone or something is wrong. Difficult people are often the cause for conflicts.

Conflicts shall be fought or avoided.

Conflicts are fought most effectively by controlling humans.

When conflicts are not handled they grow and become difficult to deal with.

A view of conflicts in domination systems

- Conflict is negative and bad.

- Therefore we should always try to avoid conflicts.

- Conflict is a sign that someone has done something wrong.

- Conflict is something that troublemakers or difficult people start, so we need to have effective ways to control people.

- Control and harmony are created by overcoming our opponent, and sometimes it must be done with some form of punishment or through violence or coercion.

The result of this approach

Conflicts that are not dealt with often escalate. This in turn gives us conflicts that are even more challenging to handle. A challenging conflict that is difficult to solve and energy consuming, seems to be proof that conflicts really are unnatural, and something we must try to avoid. When we believe that there is always a troublemaker, who for no apparent reason, is the cause of a conflict, there is the risk that we are not really aware of what can help us in handling the conflict.

If we believe that the true nature of humans is one of violence and selfishness and that it is only through controlling people that we can avoid fights, it is easy to see conflict as something that springs from this violent and selfish nature. In this case we would probably want to protect ourselves from these "destructive beings" with the help of organizations that minimize the amount of conflicts, often through control in various forms.

Statements such as: "why do you have to bring that up?", or "hey, come on, you really are in agreement, so stop fighting", can be expressions of worry about not being able to deal with conflicts. When we want to protect others from harm, our first impulse might be to try to stop the conflict, rather than trying to help the parties understand each other.

The danger with trying to soften or stop the conflict is that these actions help it instead to grow stronger until the situation becomes unsustainable. To return to a place of cooperation and trust can be a pretty big challenge if the conflict has been going on over a long period of time. People in conflicts have a need to be heard and understood, not to hear that they should not fight. When people are not understood there is a great risk that they will "scream even louder" in hopes of maybe finally being heard.

If we approach peoples' dissatisfaction with the attitude that they are really trying to find ways to meet their needs, new ways for connection and cooperation often emerge. With knowledge about how we can carry on when we are stuck, we can deal with both our own conflicts and help others to solve theirs. When we see conflicts as something enriching, our motivation to deal with them will increase.

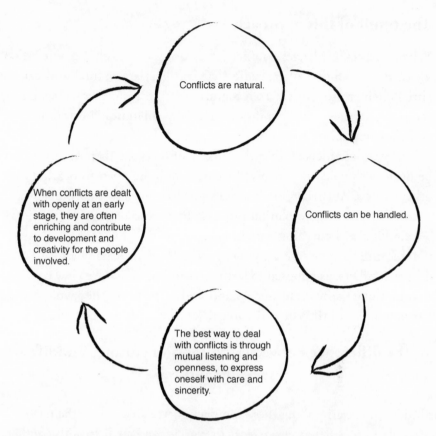

The view of conflicts in life-serving cultures

- Conflicts are natural and can be handled.

- Conflicts occur where there are strong values and dreams.

- Conflicts can be enriching and can contribute in creating new ways to cooperate.

- Conflicts contribute most if they are handled by "win-win" methods.

The result of this approach

When one acknowledges conflicts, they do not so easily become taboo. Thus, the likelihood of realizing that conflicts are natural and can be enriching increases greatly. To recognize conflicts instead of trying to hide them away, increases the conditions that they will unfold into connection and cooperation.

Deal with conflicts at an early stage. Conflicts are then most likely to be dealt with when the involved parties are more open to hearing each other's views. At this point all parties involved are able to bring new and creative ideas to the resolution process. This creativity makes it easier to see conflicts as something enriching.

Achieving harmony by denying existing conflicts usually leads to even deeper conflicts, as opposed to lasting harmony. When we view conflicts as something we want to understand and learn from, they will become less taboo. It will then be easier to get "all the cards on the table".

The difference between domination cultures and life - serving cultures

To gain more clarity about these approaches, we can compare them to each other. If these differences are clear to you, it can be a help with conflicts and mediation.

Concepts of a leader's role in conflict resolution

Domination cultures:
The leader is assumed to have control over all conflicts. This is often done by trying to push away conflicts, or by using power and violence to fight them.

Life-serving cultures:
The leader identifies and points out conflicts while also trying to support dealing with them. The leader asks for support to handle conflicts when it serves the group.

Concepts of power

Domination cultures:
Focus lies on having power over people. Those with the most power also have access to those resources that strengthen their power.

Life-serving Cultures:
Focus lies on allocating resources and power; to cooperate with people. Power is used to make sure that resources are given to the ones who are in the greatest need of them.

Concepts of cooperation

Domination cultures:
Cooperation is based on duty, guilt and shame or on "we and them-thinking" and aggression against other groups.

Life-serving Cultures:
Cooperation is based on freedom and interdependence. There is trust that humans want to contribute and cooperate if their needs are taken into consideration.

Concepts on which means to use to reach the ends

Domination cultures:
Punishment and reward is used to control people's actions and choices.

Life-serving Cultures:
Communication based on honesty and empathic listening is used to influence people. Force is used when there are direct threats of physical injury, but only to protect and never to punish.

Concepts of justice

Domination cultures:
Justice is achieved through the use of punishment and is governed by systems that decide who has done wrong. The person who has done wrong deserves his or her punishment and shall make amends for her crime.

Life-serving Cultures:
Justice is achieved through dialogue and restorative measures. To create justice without bringing people to justice. Facing danger or threats, one intervenes to protect, but never to punish.

Concepts of education and socialization

Domination cultures:

In order for we humans to serve systems based on domination, as children we must learn to work for a reward (for example praise, high grades or money). Therefore, it also becomes important that we learn what authorities (those in power of the resources) think. This makes some of us obedient and easy to control. Others rebel as a counteraction of the control, but the system almost always remains the same.

Life-serving cultures

Education and socialization is based on freedom and mutuality. One focuses both on what the individual needs and wants, as well as on how exchange can come about through mutual respect and cooperation with others. Motivation comes from within which is of maximum support for lasting and continual learning.

Win-Win or zero-sum games

"In 1964 an American father and his twelve-year-old son were enjoying a beautiful Saturday in Hyde Park, London, playing catch with a Frisbee. Few in England had seen a Frisbee at that time and a small group of strollers gathered to watch this strange sport. Finally, one Homburg-clad Britisher came over to the father: "Sorry to bother you. Been watching you a quarter of an hour. Who's winning?"[1]

We are so used to contests and focusing on who is winning, that we easily transfer this way of thinking to all areas of life. In a friendship relationship or a love relationship, few of us might consciously ask ourselves the question: "who is winning". Still, conflicts often resemble contests where our struggle for power comes down to winning over our opponent.

Mediation with the help of NVC aims to create a so called "Win-Win" solution, as opposed to a zero-sum game. A zero-sum game means that gains and losses equal out, the total sum of the gains and the losses in

---

1 Fisher, Roger & Ury, William(1987), Getting to Yes. Arrow Books Limited.

the game is zero[1]. The consequence of this is that a player can only win if someone else loses. When it comes to dealing with conflicts, the power struggle therefore seldom leads to solutions that are satisfying in the long run. A compromise is usually also a zero-sum game because the parties are giving up something to gain something else. Instead of compromising, NVC helps us to find solutions that satisfy as many needs as possible, where no one is losing because someone else is winning.

---

1 http://en.wikipedia.org/wiki/Zero-sum_(game_theory) 18 maj 09 The formal definition of zero-sum games is a game where the difference between the stake and the expected gain is zero. For example, if a lottery ticket costs $2 and the probability of winning $20 is 10%, the game is a zero-sum game. This is because the expected gain (10% of $20) is the same size as the stake. Zero-sum games don't add anything new, create no added value, only circulate money. Many kinds of lotteries are zero-sum games.

Chapter 3

Minding other peoples' business

Mediating without being invited

Many of us act as a third party in our everyday lives, often without thinking of ourselves as mediators. This can be between our children, in our family or at work. When I mediate without having been asked to do so, I intervene in a way I think will benefit everyone the most. Sometimes I use only a few words and sometimes I am more active. For example, I can "translate" something that could create misunderstanding between the involved parties into something that can be easier for everyone to hear.

In many informal mediation situations it is not clear to the parties that I intervene with the purpose of helping them to create connection. This means that I may get questioned by one or both parties. When people are used to speaking in a certain way, it can feel awkward to hear someone reformulate what they have said. Even if one realizes that the reformulation is easier for the other party to understand, it can be difficult to take in new ways of expressing oneself. However, most people appreciate when one tries to help out in a situation where they are not reaching each other, and to help without trying to make them do something that they don't want to do. You will probably be well received when you try to mediate, but I want to share some things that can be valuable to think about in situations where someone has difficulties in receiving support.

When the mediator is not received

If, without being asked to do so, I rephrase what needs I hear that one party has and then ask the other party to reflect them back, it can be perceived as a put-down. Even if I do it with caution, irritation can be directed towards me - with the demand that I don't interfere. In these cases there are at least two things I can do. I can remind myself that it can be a challenge for an upset person to appreciate that someone just wants to help, and is not there to criticize or "take sides". I can also connect with what my own purpose is behind taking the role of the third party. When I remind myself about what motivates me to intervene, it becomes easier to continue even if others struggle with seeing the beauty in what I am doing just then.

Be prepared to show both parties in a conflict that what you want to contribute with is to help them create more connection between each other. Do this first by showing that you are trying to understand how the situation affects them, and second by giving information about what you are trying to do. I suggest this order because my experience is that an irritated person will have a hard time taking in any explanations if she hasn't first been met with understanding.

In mediation words are often very useful, but empathy can also be conveyed without using words. Just to be present when two people are disagreeing, is a support for them. It helps them to slow down the tempo and contributes to their safety. Many people become more aware about how they communicate if there is a third party present. With this awareness it also becomes easier for them to communicate in a way that supports connection.

Civil courage or disrespectful behavior?

First they came for the Communists,
and I didn't speak up,
because I wasn't a Communist.
Then they came for the Jews,
and I didn't speak up,
because I wasn't a Jew.
Then they came for the Catholics,
and I didn't speak up,
because I was a Protestant.
Then they came for me,
and by that time there was no one
left to speak up for me.
Rev. Martin Niemoller, 1945 [1]

On many occasions I have heard people say:
"That's none of my business, it's their problem."
"They will have to deal with that within their family."
"It's not respectful to mediate between adults if they haven't asked for it."
I guess that for the person who makes such statements, respect, integrity and the freedom to choose are very important. Respect and integrity are important to me as well. At the same time, I feel sad when I think about

1. http://www.hoboes.com/html/FireBlade/Politics/niemoller.shtml 4 November 2008.

the above statements , because I often hear people seeing conflicts as private affairs. In my opinion, it is better to intervene "too often" than "too seldom". I would like to see more of us try to mediate when we see that people are not able to connect with each other, instead of trying to avoid it out of the fear that someone will get irritated or not like what we are doing.

If no one ever intervenes when the situation really calls for it, we have a situation of "survival of the fittest". I have seen conflicts go on for years because no one, including myself, has done anything to help the people create connection.

Passivity supports violence

Martin Luther King did not only express the famous words:
"The big tragedy is not the brutality of the evil people. The big tragedy is the good peoples' silence." [1]

He also claimed:
"You are not only responsible for what you are saying, but also for what you are not saying."

During times of peace, most violence in society occurs between people in close relationships. 88% of women who are murdered knew their murderer. Most were murdered by their present or former husband or boyfriend. In Russia, 13,000 women are murdered every year. During the ten years that Russia and Afghanistan were engaged in war, 14,000 Russian soldiers were killed. Nearly as many Russian women died through violence in their homes in one year as did men during that ten-year war. Similar numbers may hold true in other countries. In our private lives where other people do not have access to what is going on, violence often seems to be an accepted way to exercise control.

Media rarely shows the violence that exists in individual households. And too often we defend our passivity with the explanation that we "respect the private lives of others".

---

1 King, Martin Luther, Jr (2002), I've Been to the Mountaintop: From a Call to Conscience. Grand Central Publishing.

Through interviews where one tries to understand what happened during the genocide in Rwanda and in former Yugoslavia, it has become clear that the silence and passivity of the rest of the world was interpreted as consent for what was happening in those countries. In 1994, almost one million Tutsis where killed by the Hutus. It is estimated that over 120,000 Hutus took part in the killing. In reports afterwards, many of them said that they interpreted the silence of the UN as support for what they did. The passivity from the UN and other national governments was interpreted as support to eradicate the "cockroaches" (the name given to the Tutsis by the Hutus).

When I read about these events and realize how easily passivity is interpreted as consent, it becomes easier for me to choose to mediate - even when I have not been invited to do so. I can not know if a dispute that I see between two family members will lead to violence behind the locked doors of their home. Therefore, I would rather take the chance to protect someone, than to refrain from intervening out of the fear of not being well received.

Yet another example of what can happen when we relate in a passive way became clear to me when I read Katarina Wennstam's book "A Real Rapist". Wennstam has studied gang rapes in Sweden, and has tried to clarify why certain girls were raped. The studies showed that the girls who were victims of gang rape often had a given reputation. They were girls who were called "whores" or "sluts". They were girls who according to their "reputation" were talked about as being "willing to have sex with anyone", or "just asking for trouble" and so on. Even adults in the girls' environment contributed to these labels and interpretations, and used them themselves. They also interpreted the girls' choice of clothing as slutty, and linked this to the same type of language. These adults contributed to the violence by being passive and not challenging how the labels and claims about the girls were spread. The studies showed that some of these girls were actually virgins before they were raped, but their reputation told a different story.

I hope that everyone who reads this can see the value of spending time helping both youth and adults to talk about labels and to deal with static images of each other. The importance of this is further reinforced by the studies in Wennstam's book that show that only in those occasions when a gang rape occurred involving a girl without labels, the boys changed

A Helping Hand
Mediation with Nonviolent Communication

schools afterward. This, because they were so hard-pressed by their peers that it became impossible for them to stay in their school. However, in the rape of girls with labels, the girls were the ones who almost always changed schools. Among those who tried to stay, the labels and evaluations often became even stronger after the horror that they had been through.

Passivity and obedience

The Milgram experiment is a series of well-known experiments within the field of Social Psychology. The purpose of the experiments was to examine a volunteer's tendency to obey an authority who instructed them to take actions that their conscience would normally not allow them to take. The experiment was first described in 1963 by Stanley Milgram, psychologist at Yale University.

"The legal and philosophic aspects of obedience are of enormous import, but an empirically grounded scientist eventually comes to the point where he wishes to move from abstract discourse to the careful observation of concrete instances. In order to take a close look at the act of obeying, I set up a simple experiment at Yale University. Eventually, the experiment was to involve more than a thousand participants and would be repeated at several universities, but at the beginning, the conception was simple. A person comes to a psychological laboratory and is told to carry out a series of acts that come increasingly into conflict with conscience. The main question is how far the participant will comply with the experimenter's instructions before refusing to carry out the actions required of him."

The experiment leader ordered the teacher/volunteer to give an electric shock to the student each time the student answered incorrectly the questions that the teacher/volunteer read out loud. The teacher/volunteer pressed buttons that would provide an electrical shock, but in reality the student did not actually receive a shock. In fact, the student was an actor who was completely clear about the purpose of the experiment, and only pretended to be receiving an electric shock.

The experiment began with the experiment leader explaining that they would be testing the effect of punishments on learning. The teacher/volunteer, received an electric shock of 45 volts to demonstrate the shocks that the "student" would be exposed to during the course of the experiment. If the answer was wrong, the student received an electrical shock.

The strength of the shock was increased by each wrong answer.

As the intensity of the shocks increased, the student complained increasingly loudly, banged on the wall, until finally falling silent, neither giving further responses nor complaints. By then, many volunteers wanted to discontinue the experiment and see how the student was doing. When the electrical shocks reached 135 volts, some volunteers paused and questioned the experiment. But several of them went on even further, after having been assured that they were not responsible for what happened to the "student". Some volunteers began to laugh nervously or show other signs of extreme stress when the "student" expressed increasing pain. Whenever the volunteers said that they wanted to cancel the experiment, they were urged to continue. In cases where the volunteer, despite fairly persistent persuasion attempts, wanted to stop, the experiment was brought to an end. Otherwise, the experiment was cancelled only when the volunteer had given the strongest possible shock of 450 volts, three times in succession.

In the first series, 65% of the volunteers (26 of 40) gave the maximum electrical shock in the experiment, even though many were very uncomfortable and showed clear stress syndrome. All volunteers questioned the experiment at some point. All continued giving electrical shocks past the 300 volt point. When other researchers repeated the experiment after Milgram, they got similar results.

The results in Milgram's classic experiment have often been interpreted as having to do with how well we are trained to obey authority. Something that I think is particularly interesting is what happened when the tests were conducted with one extra person in the room, in addition to the experiment leader and the volunteer. When the volunteer protested and was persuaded by the experiment leader (authority) to continue, the other person said that the volunteer was free to cancel if he or she did not want to continue. In these cases the volunteer stopped giving electrical shocks far sooner than in the other cases.

Given what happened in the experiment when there wasn't anyone trying to influence the student, I want to illustrate the opportunities we have to influence events that we may not believe we have the power to influence. Regardless of whether what happened during these experiments was about obedience or about following the norm, the experiments remind me of the importance of acting, rather than being a passive spectator to violence and destructive group processes.

I hope that this gives you an extra boost in your desire to mediate within a context where it feels a little uncomfortable, but where it could make a difference.

Your internal reaction when people around you are in conflict

Purpose: To reflect on and become attentive of your own inner dialogue during conflicts, so that you can be more aware of the way you want to act. The questions below are ways to support your reflection in a constructive way.

Write down your answers so that you support a deeper reflection. Be aware of how you think when people around you are in conflict. Give extra attention to thoughts that make you less disposed to mediate when you are not invited. They can be thoughts that sound something like this:

"It is up to them to find a solution... "
"I should not interfer."
"I hope they will not yell at me that way as well!"

a. What needs of yours are not being met when you relate to the situation in this way?

b. What needs of yours are you trying to meet when you think in this way?

c. What needs of both parties would you like to try to meet by thinking in this way?

d. Which of their needs may not be met with the way you are thinking or acting?

e. How would you want to act or think in a similar situation in the future?

Your internal reaction to other peoples' conflicts when you want to give advice or "fix it"

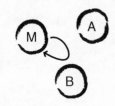

Purpose: To reflect on and become attentive to your own
inner dialogue, when you want to give advice or try to fix someone 's
conflict, so you can be more aware of how you want to act. The questions
below are a way to support you in reflecting in a constructive way. Write
down your answers if this will support your reflection. Some of us choose
neither to be passive spectators nor to mediate when we see conflict. Instead
we put on a "fixing-hat" as soon as we "sniff" dissidence. Maybe we are
trying to solve the conflict for the parties, to mitigate it, to calm someone
down or to give advice on how those involved can handle the situation. If
you recognise yourself in this description, reflect more deeply upon what
is happening the next time you are with people who are not in agreement
with each other. Or remember the last time you were in a conflict. What
is going on inside of you? Do you recognize thoughts like:

> *"They should not argue about this!"*
> *"This is a trifle that can easily be solved by…"*
> *"If they only understood that they have to express themselves in other*
> *ways, if they could only stop…then everything would be solved."*

a. What needs of yours are you trying to meet when you think in this
   way?

b. What needs of yours are not met when you relate to the situation
   in this way?

c. How would you like to approach a similar situation in the future?

Chapter 4

Sweet revenge and losing face

How revenge became sweet

"To be bitter is to is take poison, hoping that someone else will die."
Carolyn Myss[1]

We can see vengeance and the desire for revenge as an expression of the need for empathy. There are many similarities between revenge and mediation because both strategies aim to recreate a kind of balance, contribute to self-respect and resolve a conflict.

Although revenge is a tragic and ineffective way to meet the need for empathy, I see it as an attempt to gain understanding of how much one has suffered. One who takes revenge upon someone also wants to retain his or her self-respect and create balance in the relationship. They often "overdo" their revenge, in hopes of scaring the other party and discouraging further revenge.

Revenge is built upon the idea that the other party has done something wrong as well as the attitude that the person who does something wrong deserves punishment. Revenge easily escalates and turns into a spiral of revenge that no one knows how to get out of. The parties keep the spiral swirling through their actions. Both parties take the same position: "I know what is right", or "I have justice on my side." In the spiral of revenge, the "victim" and the "perpetrator" change places; first the "perpetrator" becomes the "victim" and then they change places again and again in a never-ending process.

I think we retaliate because we have learned to do so, not because it is in our nature to do this. We have also learned to be "entertained" by violence, for example in movies whose message is based on the idea that violence leads to peace. "The evil ones" get what they deserve because they have done something wrong. "The good ones" practically do "the evil ones" a favor by punishing them, because they give them a chance to understand that they have done something wrong and should change their ways. They have now been given the punishment they deserve and, according to the myth that violence leads to harmony, the situation will be settled when the punishment has been experienced.

I have never stopped being amazed over the trust we have in the process of finding scapegoats. Through movies with explicit "bad guys", such as

1 Myss, Caroline (1997), Anatomy of the spirit. Three Rivers Press.

those in the Bond movies, Terminator or Kill Bill, our belief is strengthened that an opponent will want to take revenge when things are not going their way. The violence of entertainment relies on the idea that the "villain" will want revenge at any sign of difficulties. This learned myth of violence and revenge makes it difficult for us to connect with our natural compassion. When we want revenge we are actually longing for inner peace, but are not clear about the limitations involved in this choice of strategy.

One difference between revenge and mediation is that in mediation we try to care for everyone's needs, not just for one side's needs. It is not only my needs that are important, but your needs as well. We don't want to ignore what is important for any one of the parties, but rather provide alternatives to revenge. Mediation can restore mutual respect and real balance, instead of the endless suffering that is brought forth through revenge. The notion that we live in a world where "as you sow, so shall you reap" easily pacifies us. With this approach it is easy to think that the one who is punished has probably done something to deserve it. This approach can lead us to passively witness, even over a long period of time, someone creating pain for others.

Revenge and forgiveness – two sides of the same coin

Revenge and forgiveness have some similarities, but also important differences. I have many memories from my childhood of how the concept of forgiveness was used in a way that rarely led to what it was intended to accomplish. To forgive usually meant that someone wanted to put an end to a situation and leave it behind them.

Although I am virtually "allergic" to the approach towards forgiveness that I was introduced to as a child, I know that for many people, forgiveness is very essential and has many levels of depth. As a child, "sorry" was a word one was supposed to say to make things right. By some kind of magic, this word was supposed to repair whatever had been damaged. In this approach towards "forgiveness", the intention is to get people to pay for their sins, suffer and feel deep remorse, thereby changing their behavior. It is based on the belief that people need to realize how bad they are in order to fully understand how their actions don't contribute to others. Therefore, "sorry" is one of the first things a child in a culture of domination must learn to say properly. (I hope that at least some of you do not recognize yourself in the cartoon below!)

Some people also attach great importance and prestige to being a person who can forgive. They want to forgive, even if the other person does not repent. If we have learned that "good people forgive others when they have done something wrong", we might find that we have forgiven without actually having experienced reconciliation about what has happened. This "forgiveness" is also based on the idea that there is a right and a wrong. It creates a power imbalance in the relationship, where one is seen as "the good one" who forgives and the other as the "sinful" or "the evil one", who is forgiven.

A common way to try to manage conflicts in our culture is to apologize or

forgive and, in many cases, this becomes quite absurd. First I do something that is painful for another person and then they must forgive me. To first be hurt by someone, who then asks for forgiveness, can feel like an insult. An apology in this situation does not mean very much for the person who has been hurt, even if it is sincerely meant.

Many of us have learned to apologize rather mechanically (thanks to experiments similar to those in the pictures on the previous page) and not because we have really realized how painful the effects of our actions have been for others.

The similarity between revenge and superficial forgiveness is that they are both one-sided. Whether we take revenge or express an automatic "sorry", we are not focusing on ways to try to relate to what has happened. When we try to relate to what has happened, we can find ways to allow everyone to have their needs met. The one who desires to take revenge wants to show the other that what happened was wrong, unjust or abnormal. The one who desires forgiveness wishes to draw a line over what has happened, forget it and move on. Though many needs are not met by this course of action. What is tragic about this approach, is that it reduces our chances of learning something from the situation. If we confuse reconciliation with superficial forgiveness, there is a great risk that we will miss the opportunity to truly repair what has happened.

If we forgive because it seems like a good idea or "the right thing to do", we choose to move forward willingly (or at least so it may seem) without having our needs met.

If we forgive in order to avoid dealing with the unpleasant situations that might occur when we stand up for ourselves, there is the risk that bitterness will gradually catch up with us later.

If we think it is noble to forgive, to "be a good human being" and not because we really have been through a process of forgiveness, there is a risk that it will lead to a more superficial connection.

When we forgive without experiencing this inner shift it instead leads to greater distance and bitterness. I have seen many examples where someone has "given her or his forgiveness", though he or she still felt great bitterness about what had happened. With sadness, I have seen how it led to resistance towards gaining a deeper connection or cooperation with the other person.

An important difference between the two strategies; forgiveness without reconciliation having actually been carried out and revenge, is that the person who wants revenge continues to act, and does not let go of the conflict. The avenger says:

"You have misbehaved and I will not forget this."

The one who forgives without being really fully ready to move on says: *"What you have done is wrong but I will overlook it."*

If we use NVC, we neither want to be satisfied with superficial forgiveness in the form of "overlooking things", nor with revenge. Instead of a superficial "I'm sorry", we want to create deep, mutual reconciliation.

When we are not just trying to move forward, but also want the other person to really take in how his or her actions have affected us, we give ourselves a chance to thoroughly reconcile with what has happened. At the same time, we are giving the other person a chance to understand and reconcile with his or her choices.

The times when a person fully takes in the fact that he or she has done something that has not satisfied the needs of the other person and mourns this, there is a chance to repair both the person's self-respect and trust in the relationship.

The core of mediation, revenge and reconciliation

In order for parties to experience a mediation talk as meaningful, the parties need to be able to experience what they might have hoped to experience through revenge or apologies. For example, it can be about the needs for calmness and quiet, respect or the need to be heard.

Imagine a situation where one party says that he or she just wants to move ahead and therefore wants to end the mediation. As a mediator, you are unsure if this person really has had a deep experience of reconciliation with what has happened. Because it can harm the relationship to end mediation at this point, it is very useful for you as mediator to pay attention to what is happening. Once you understand the situation, connect with what needs the person wants to meet by not talking any further about the conflict. If the conflict has been going on over a long period of time, the person can, for example, have a strong desire for peace and quiet and therefore wants the mediation to come to a close. There are other ways of contributing to peace and quiet, for example by taking a break or by lowering the tempo of the dialogue.

In situations where someone would like to make peace with something and their needs have been painfully unmet by the actions of another person, and where there is no possibility for a reconciliation conversation with the other person Marshall Rosenberg has developed a special "healing process"[1]. This situation could be because the other person is sick, far away, not willing to participate or even dead. Though beyond the scope of this book, the process is partially described in chapter 9, where a mediator or two mediators "play" a role in the mediation talk.

Empathy instead of "forgive me"

When we have made a mistake, we can use the principles of NVC to apologize in a different way than many of us are familiar with. First, we listen with empathy until the other person feels completely understood in how our actions have done has affected him or her. Second, we try to take in what the other person is saying and express how it affects us to hear it. Then we tell them if we are mourning the choices that we made, and that we understand what consequences our actions had for the other person.

Thereafter, the other person usually wants to hear why we acted as we did; in other words, what needs we were trying to meet by acting so.

Unfortunately, an apology that does not contain these three parts can be experienced as trying to "smooth over" what has happened, rather than to create reconciliation. If the apology is to have any effect, it must therefore mean that I am truly willing to accept how my choices have affected the other person, and that I am willing to contribute to reconciliation in some way.

To apologize with the help of NVC greatly facilitates conflict resolution. A mediator can help to clarify apologies and to contribute to reconciliation between the parties.

---

1 Rosenberg, Marshall (2004) Getting Past the Pain Between Us. Puddle Dancer Press

A Helping Hand
Mediation with Nonviolent Communication

To apologize with the help of NVC

Step 1. Listen with empathy and try to really take in how your actions have affected the other person.

Step 2. When you have taken in what has been said, express what is going on in you when you understand how your actions affected the other person.

Step 3. Tell what needs you where trying to meet through your actions. Express what motivated you, even if you would have chosen to do it differently now that you have realized the consequences.

Losing face

"He is just doing that in order not to lose face" is an expression that sometimes is used to suggest that there is something wrong with wanting to "save face". What does "saving face" actually mean? That someone cares about his or her experience of self-respect? That someone is ashamed and wants to protect their inner dignity? Does the person perhaps feel fear and worry about not being a part of the community if he or she is "exposed"?

To describe what it means to "lose face" helps us to see the situation more clearly. We do this by paying attention to what we see or hear in the very instant we make the interpretation "he is afraid of losing face". So what can it mean?:

- Being caught doing something that we have denied we have done or are doing and to feel guilt and shame about it.

- Admitting something that we have thus far been denying or felt shame about.

- Trying to hide disappointment, fear, grief or other strong feelings in the presence of others and not succeeding.

- Being caught having distorted facts or avoided sharing some essential information.

There may be many reasons why you do not want to be open and to share how you have been affected in a conflict, or what has occurred prior to a mediation. However, when someone is holding back important information that affects the core of the conflict, it will most likely affect the outcome of the mediation in a negative way.

If someone does not want to share with others something you as a mediator imagine would support the connection and the conflict resolution, you need first to show that you are willing to try to understand how difficult it is for one or several parties to share this. You respond to their concerns with empathy. Only when they have been understood do you remind them that if they are not willing to express what is going on within them, it will be difficult to move forward. You can clarify that mediation is based on "putting all the cards on the table" in order to find solutions that will satisfy everyone's needs (including their own). Watch out that you don't do this in a way that sounds like a demand or a reprimand.

What you want is to give the parties involved a chance to see how the result of the mediation is affected by their willingness to share openly or not.

For example, it can be expressed like this:

"A certain degree of transparency is crucial for mediation to work and I hear that it is a challenge for you to share how you experience the situation. Therefore, I wonder if there is anything I or anyone else can do that can help you talk more openly about what you are interested in and what you want to see happen?"

Or:

"I hear that it is a challenge for you to share what is going on in you. It makes me a little worried because mediation is based on sharing what we need and want. I am wondering whether mediation is the best way to move forward. Would you like us all to consider how both of you could proceed in any other way?"

Another chance to move beyond interpretations around "losing face", is to get in touch with the needs one is hoping to meet through interpreting the situation. Some examples below

Person A says about person B:
"He is just trying to avoid losing face, it's just manipulation, trying to escape

his responsibilities."

I guess that person A is needing connection, honesty or trust.
Person B says about person A:
"She is just trying to push me into saying things that I will later regret having said."

I guess that person B may have a need for respect, integrity and care. Your role as a mediator is to ensure that both sides are heard, so you could continue like this.

"A, do you want it to be heard that for you, honesty is incredibly important, as well as being able to trust that what is said is followed up on?

(Turning to person B) *"Is it that for you, honesty is also important, but you also want to experience integrity and care when someone is expressing something?"*

In a system based on domination and ranking, the approach is to make people feel really badly about themselves in order to make them change their ways. Therefore, low self-respect or even self-hatred would be a positive driving force behind this change. If one party chooses to relate from this approach, it can be a challenge for you as a mediator, since that person will often resort to imposing guilt and verbal attacks when something gets too painful.

As a mediator using NVC, I want to protect the parties from hearing criticism, threats or demands. I act out of the assumption that we are most willing to change when we see how new choices contribute to better satisfying everyone's needs. Thus, I am trying to help the parties to hear each other's needs so that they see the humanity in one another, instead of trying to determine who has done right or who has done wrong.

When we mourn what we have done, with the understanding that we did the best we were able to do in that moment, we can be led towards new creative ways to satisfy our own needs as well as the needs of the other party. Therefore, your role as a mediator is to focus on the universal needs that the parties are trying to express and to help them maintain their self-respect. The parties can then jointly come up with what they want to change in order to meet everyone's needs, or at the very least, take them into consideration.

What do you do to avoid losing face?

1. What do you do, or what might you sometimes do, to "save face"?

2. Which of your needs are you trying to meet by doing this?

3. What do you see others do, or hear them say, that you would consider as "losing face"?

4. Which of their needs do you think are not being met at that moment?

Never do anything to avoid shame or guilt

It is possible to learn a great deal from exploring shame and guilt. When I freely choose to explore what it means to feel guilt and shame, it is very different from someone else blaming me or trying to stimulate shame in me. As a mediator I do not want anyone to feel shame or guilt, since it leads to increased resistance.

As a mediator, it is also important to remember how uncomfortable it can be for people to feel shame or guilt. Shame is the essence of "losing face". Some people will do almost anything to avoid experiencing both shame and guilt. This discomfort creates a strong resistance towards the idea of talking about "what I have done" or attempting to repair it. To do so means standing face to face with shame.

To experience strong feelings of shame can be an obstacle in mediation. A person who is experiencing shame is often quiet and responds only to direct questions. He or she can go along with almost any kind of agreement just to put an end to the mediation. At such times it is valuable to take a break or to spend some time alone with that person. To fully experience being heard with empathy in the shame one is experiencing creates the inner space needed to choose more openness. It provides relief and well-wanted distance in a situation where shame could otherwise completely paralyze oneself.

One of my friends heard Marshall Rosenberg say, "don't do anything to avoid guilt and shame." She was puzzled by this and on several occasions we talked about what he really wanted to say. Then one evening when she was visiting me, she suddenly realized what he meant.

As it started to get late, she found herself thinking:

"I have to go home now, because my husband is waiting for me." Suddenly, she realized that she was about to leave in order to avoid shame. She understood as well that her husband, without having done anything, would have to "pay" if she went home only because she thought she had to. She would be annoyed because he "demanded" that she come home, even though he had not actually demanded it. Our relationships always suffer when we associate them with shame or guilt.

She explored the difference between going home based on the idea that she "should" do it and going home because she really wanted to be with her husband.

Her feelings of guilt reminded her that she wanted to contribute to his well-being, while at the same time wanting to choose exactly when she wanted to do it.

When my friend later left for home, she did it with a hopeful openness about how she would be able to handle any possible bitter mood in her husband. If we do things out of the joy of contributing to others, rather than out of a sense of duty, we will enrich our relationships.

Our need to contribute to others usually lies behind our feelings of shame and guilt. At the same time, we have other present needs wanting to be satisfied. Here, our "internal mediator" is given the task of trying to find new ways to act with the potential to satisfy all needs.

Chapter 5

Nonviolent Communication as an approach to mediation

Nonviolent Communication

"Nonviolent Communication is really an integration of a certain spirituality in our daily lives, our relationships, and our political activities."
Marshall Rosenberg[1]

Nonviolent Communication (NVC) is a combination of a way of thinking, a way of communicating and a way to use the power we have in a particular way. The purpose of NVC is to create a quality of connection between us that will bring to life our will to try to satisfy everyone's needs. In this approach, everyone's needs are valued. Mutual respect and choice are key concepts as they are needed both when we want to achieve effective cooperation, and when we want to handle conflicts.

As a mediator, you can use the principles and tools of NVC without the participants in the mediation being familiar with these principles. NVC supports you in focusing primarily on creating connection between the parties. For example, you can do this by:

- Supporting them in honestly expressing their own needs, dreams and interests.

- Encouraging them to listen for each other's desires, needs, interests and dreams, regardless of how the other is expressing them.

- Listening with empathy until they are ready to listen to each other's needs, feelings, dreams, interests and wishes.

Only when this human connection has been established, does a mediator using NVC focus on how the conflict can be solved. If we try to come up with solutions before we are clear about what the parties need, we run the risk of missing important needs when choosing how to resolve the conflict. Of course, we want to find a satisfying solution that, to the maximum extent possible, satisfies everyone's needs and is sustainable in the future. Genuine cooperation only takes place when everyone trusts that all parties will care for everyone's needs and values with respect.

---

1 Rosenberg, Marshall (2005), *Speak Peace In A World Of Conflict, What You Say Next Will Change Your World.* Puddle Dancer Press.

Focus conflict resolution and meditation first on:

1. Connection, by drawing attention to feelings and needs.

2. Willingness to contribute, which awakens in people when they are connected with each other's needs and humanity.

Then focus on:

1. Understanding the cause of the problem.

2. The solution to the problem.

Even if a person is expressing his or her needs in the form of threats, demands, labels, bias, diagnosis or analysis, we can choose to listen for what he or she needs and longs for. When we listen for what a person needs, we gain a deeper sense of what he or she values, which can help us to understand and awaken our natural compassion.

The most important thing for parties in conflict to express and be heard in, is what is going on inside them. People who are upset have a deeper longing for someone to understand their feelings and needs than for someone to understand exactly what has happened.

At the beginning of a mediation, people are seldom very open about what they feel. They are often more ready to "fight for their cause", than to reveal themselves before their opponent. When someone is defending themselves or blaming the other, the conflict resolution is made more difficult. To minimize the risk of someone becoming defensive, the mediator helps the parties to express what they are feeling and needing.

Basic principles of NVC

NVC can easily be seen as just a way to communicate. However, this way of communicating is an attempt to reflect various basic principles. These principles underlie the whole approach. Here are two principles that I use for strengthening my ability to communicate with other people with the help of NVC:

1. It is easier to create connection between people if we assume that everything people do, they do with the intention of trying to meet their needs.

2. It is easier to create cooperation and connection with other people if we assume that they want to contribute to others when they feel that it is voluntary.

NVC can be used both for trying to understand what has happened when a conflict occurs, as well as in managing the conflict. In both cases, it is important to consider the needs of both sides. People in a conflict often take a stand only for what they themselves need and want, because they believe that winning over the other party will get their needs met. This is why one of the mediator's tasks is to focus on both sides.

A few years ago I saw a headline in a weekly newspaper that read: "How to win every argument!" The title reminded me of mediations I have done between couples where the conflict has looked a lot like a contest or a power struggle. We are so used to competing that we do so even in our closest relationships. We long for others to understand what is important of us, but through competing we create an opposing effect, which leaves our needs even further unmet.

Using the principles of NVC, we can find ways out of fixed positions by first focusing on creating connection between the parties. When we are fully connected with someone, it is like a kind of natural law for our compassion to eventually be awakened and with it our desire to try to satisfy even the other's needs. The mediator highlights what can create more connection between the parties. The basic principles of NVC are used in the same way in mediation as in when we are trying to handle a conflict that we ourselves are involved in. What separates these situations is that during a mediation we "lend out" our ability and knowledge about what creates connection, rather than just using it ourselves. To a large extent, mediation is about hearing the feelings and needs that are expressed. It means helping the parties to translate judgments into feelings and needs. As a mediator, I interrupt when I hear language based on whether or not someone deserves something, thoughts about right and wrong, demands and labels, and translate these into feelings and needs.

Moreover, it is important to remember that the mediator first and foremost focuses on helping the parties to experience connection with each other and not to himself or herself. At the same time, the mediator is also a human being with feelings and needs, which, if they are expressed, can add much to the mediation.

It is easy for the mediator to begin to take responsibility for and try to control the results of the mediation. The mediator's role is not to arrive at solutions or compromises. One of my goals as a mediator is to maximize both parties' ability to make decisions.

The mediator may of course take part in finding solutions, but does not focus on this before a connection between the parties is established. Although as a mediator I largely control the actual process of the mediation, I try as much as possible to let the solutions come from the parties themselves. I believe that the parties in a conflict have a better ability to make good decisions about something that affects them both, than any outside authority. When both parties understand each other and feel that the other wants to try to satisfy his or her needs, they will find solutions together. People are also more inclined to stick to agreements that they themselves have been responsible for creating.

After a mediation, the parties have hopefully also learned something about how they can communicate to create connection, which can help them to handle conflicts in the future.

When mediation can be used

NVC can be used to handle different kinds of conflicts. Of the four areas below, this book focuses primarily on the last two, but does touch on the first two areas.

1. Inner conflicts

Situations where you are torn between different options or ways of approaching something. For a mediator, this might mean strong doubts about one's ability to contribute.

2. Outer conflicts

When you are part of a conflict.

3. Informal mediation

When someone mediates a conflict without being asked to do so. This may be a conflict between one's children, friends or work colleagues.

4. Formal mediation

A situation where someone has been asked to act as third party (mediator) to deal with a conflict.

Mediation can be used in conflicts

1. Between neighbors
2: In business
3: At work
4: Regarding bullying or other conflicts at school
5: In family or relationship problems
6: Between landlord and tenant
7: In restorative justice
8: Between countries

The model

Clearly expressing how I am without blaming or criticizing

Empathically receiving how you are without hearing blame or criticism

Observations

What I observe (see, hear, remember, imagine, free from my evaluations) that does or does not contribute to my well-being:

What you observe (see, hear, remember, imagine, free from your evaluations) that does or does not contribute to your well-being:

"When I (see, hear)..."

"When you see/hear..."
(Sometimes unspoken when offering empathy)

Feeling

How I feel (emotion or sensation rather than thought) in relation to what I observe:

How you feel (emotion or sensation rather than thought) in relation to what you observe:

"I feel ..."

"You feel...?"

Need

What I need or value (rather than a preference, or a specific action) that causes my feelings:

What you need or value (rather than a preference, or a specific action) that causes your feelings:

"Because I need/value..."

"because you need/value...?"

Request

The concrete actions I would like taken:

The concrete actions you would like taken:

"Would you be willing to ...?"

"Would you like ...?"
(Sometimes unspoken when offering empathy)

© Marshall Rosenberg, more info about Marshall Rosenberg or Center for Nonviolent Communication visite www.cnvc.org

A Helping Hand
Mediation with Nonviolent Communication

Needs - our common denominator

Observation, feeling, need and request are the four main components of NVC. We begin with the most central, needs.

The mediator listens for both parties' needs because all of us are equal on the level of needs. I sometimes refer to needs as our closest common denominator. Through them we can recognize ourselves in each other - which can awaken natural compassion and understanding. It increases our understanding for what is behind someone's behavior. We have the same needs, even if we choose different ways to meet them. Needs can be described as driving forces that are universal; they are shared by all people, regardless of gender, culture, age, religious or political background. It is important that the mediator distinguishes between needs and the specific strategies used to satisfy them. In addition to our physical needs, we all need, for example acceptance, freedom, community and meaning. Marshall Rosenberg summarizes his view on needs:

Needs, as I use the term, can be thought of as resources life requires to sustain itself. For example, our physical well-being depends on our needs for air, water, rest, and food being fulfilled. Our psychological and spiritual well-being is enhanced when our needs for understanding, support, honesty, and meaning are fulfilled.[1]

Cause or stimulus

When people believe that they are the reason for someone else's pain, it is easy for them to hear others' emotional expressions as criticism and to stop listening. Therefore, one important aspect of mediation is to connect what someone feels to what they need. This makes it easier for others to hear with empathy what is said, and to take responsibility for their own feelings.

For a long time, my friend had been irritated by something that one of his teenage sons was doing. When the son came home, he threw his shoes and jacket in a heap just inside the door, and his friends did the same. Sometimes, the heap grew into a small mountain (at least in my friend's eyes). Each time the pile was there he would feel the anger building up

1 Rosenberg, Marshall (2008), *We Can Work it Out*. Puddle Dancer Press.

inside. The comments he made concerning this behavior often started a quarrel between him and his son.

One day while driving home he heard on the radio that there had been a severe accident near his home. Several teenagers his son's age had been injured.

You can guess how he felt when he, a few minutes later, tripped over the usual pile of clothing and heard the teenagers upstairs! In that moment, it became clear to him that it was never the pile of clothing that caused his anger, because this time that same pile led to a feeling of relief, rather than anger.

Until then, he had not been aware that it was his own thoughts about his son that made him angry. His thoughts could have been judgments about his son, such as how he was careless or selfish. They could also have been about what he thought his son should learn about caring for others, and doing as his parents asked him to do.

When he could distinguish between his interpretations of what had happened, and from what had actually happened, it was easier to identify which needs he had. When he realized that no one else was the cause of his feelings, he experienced more freedom to act in new ways to meet his needs.

Some of our common human needs

Food, air, water
safety, movement

Interdependence

Autonomy- to choose my own dreams and how I want to reach them

To contribute
Acceptance
Respect
Support

Integrity
Trust
Creativity
Meaning

Closeness
Community
Care
Empathy
Honesty
Love

Peace, Harmony
Balance, Beauty
Inspiration
Fun

Warmth
Understanding
To be seen and heard

Feelings – the children of needs

When I use the word feelings in this book, I refer to sensations that are felt in the body. Simply describing what we feel in our bodies makes it easier to use feelings as information about what we need. If we take responsibility for our feelings by linking them to our own needs, we reduce the risk of having our emotional expressions be perceived as criticism.

Sometimes we express what we feel with words that also include what we think someone else has done. This can lead to others hearing what we say as criticism. Some examples might be when we say we feel manipulated, abused, or ignored.

To further clarify the relationship between our feelings and needs we can use a metaphor; our feelings are like the oil light on a car. The flashing light is a signal that the engine needs oil. The oil light itself is not so important, but what it warns about is very important. The information it provides helps us to do what is needed in order to prevent the engine from breaking down. Similarly, all feelings tell us about what we need. For example, when we are thirsty, we need something to drink. If we are feeling lonely, we may need community. Boredom is an opportunity to connect with our need for meaning or stimulation. When we do not listen to what we feel, we risk missing vital signs that can help us enjoy our lives.

When other people connect with what you are feeling, it makes it easier for them to relate to you because they recognize themselves in your common humanity and can put themselves in your shoes.

Feelings have a big impact on us even when they are not expressed. Imagine that someone in your workgroup or family is experiencing strong feelings. It can be seen in their body language, in their facial expression and gestures. If they are asked about what is going on within them they may reply, "nothing special". The less clear it is what a person is feeling, the more others pay attention, often unconsciously, to what might be going on in that person.

With a greater ability to express what we feel and to take responsibility for our feelings, cooperation with others will not be so hindered by those feelings. In order to maximize the odds of creating connection with the quality we are trying to achieve during mediation, focus on linking all feelings to needs.

In some contexts it may be taboo to express feelings. If the mediator chooses to put words to feelings in these situations, the parties might choose to show even less of their feelings and reactions. In cases where you notice this, you can silently notice what feelings are going on and just put words to the needs of the parties. When you choose not to put words to feelings, it is important that you pay attention to whether or not this leads to a superficial connection between the parties. If so, the conflict might become more difficult to handle.

In other situations even the use of the words "feelings" and "needs" may be inappropriate. It is useful, therefore, to have ways to express yourself around feelings and needs, without having to use these actual words. Even if you are not pronouncing the word "needs", it is enormously useful to have a focus on the needs and to inspire others to also have this. Here are some options:

"Is what is important for you to ...?"
"Is what matters to you to ...?"

"What you are longing for, is it to ...?"

"What I hear as the essence of this for you, is it to...?"

For more suggestions, see the end of this book under the title "Everyday expressions for needs".

Strong feelings - a help or a hindrance?

During a mediation, things can get pretty intense. It is therefore important for you as a mediator, to be able to deal with strong emotions. The first step in learning to deal with others' strong emotions is to know how you react when, for example, someone raises their voice or starts to cry. We often have an opportunity to practice this when we least expect it. When it happens, take a deep breath and notice what feelings it evokes in you. A possible problem is not the strong feelings of others, but rather your reaction to these feelings. The advantage here is that your own emotional reactions are something that you can do something about, while others can choose how they deal with their own feelings.

Remember that it is difficult for people to determine whether what they express during mediation is helpful or not. For instance, sometimes people get connected with something that affects them deeply and which would make a difference if they expressed it. However, they will choose to go back to the original "story", instead of sharing what has affected them. Sometimes people go back to the "story" out of habit or out of fear about not feeling completely secure with what is new. In this situation the mediator can be of great support both by listening to this insecurity and by making it clear that their strong emotions can actually contribute to the mediation process.

I was very nervous before my first task as a mediator. I was going to mediate in a conflict where relations and long-term collaborations were at stake. It was only when I fully realized that my role as a mediator was not to resolve the conflict or have the parties agree that I could relax.

To this day, I still feel a certain amount of nervousness, yet I now appreciate this feeling. Feeling nervous makes me alert and aware that I want to take the task seriously, without taking responsibility for things that I do not have to power over.

Some basic feelings we all have

Feelings when needs are fulfilled

Amazed	Fulfilled	Joyous	Stimulated
Comfortable	Glad	Moved	Surprised
Confident	Hopeful	Optimistic	Thankful
Eager	Inspired	Proud	Touched
Energetic	Intrigued	Relieved	Trustful

Feelings when needs are not fullfilled

Angry	Discouraged	Hopeless	Overwhelmed
Annoyed	Distressed	Impatient	Puzzled
Concerned	Embarrassed	Irritated	Reluctant
Confused	Frustrated	Lonely	Sad
Disappointed	Helpless	Nervous	Uncomfortable

When it comes to making
requests in mediation

One of the main components of NVC is to express concrete requests by asking for things that can help us meet our needs. When we ask for something, we want to be as specific as possible so that it is easy for others to understand what we are asking for. We also want to make sure that what we ask for is actually possible to accomplish.

The following dialogue is a sad example from a previous love relationship, where I used the word "to listen" as if it gave a concrete description about what I wanted him to do. This dialogue took place quite often:

"I want you to listen to me!"

"I am listening."

"No, you're not."

"Yes, I am!"

"Like right now, you are not listening, you don't even hear what I am saying."

Do you recognize yourself? Here, it is easy to blame one of us, instead of seeing that we both could be clearer about what we want. Some of you readers might be thinking: "How typical, men never listen." Some others might be thinking: "How typical, women always like to talk about themselves."

These evaluations are seldom helpful in doing something about the situation. For me, it is more interesting to learn from the situation and find new ways to relate, rather than to focus on who has done wrong or on preconceptions about men or women. It is clear to me now that in this situation I was not specific enough about what I wanted. Unfortunately, it did not become clear to me until long after the relationship had ended. It is not concrete enough to ask someone to "listen" if you want the other person to really know what you want from him or her.

So what could I have said instead, if I wanted to maximize the chance that he would act as I wished?

Here is an example:

"I want to tell you about something I've been through today and would like it if you sat down with me for 10 minutes and listened to me, would you like that?"

And what could my partner have said if he had wanted to see some change in the situation?

"I feel confused when I hear you say that I do not listen, because according to me I am listening. I understand that I am doing it in a way that does not help you, so would you say more about what it is that you want me to do?"

When connection and understanding has been established during a mediation, you as a mediator shift your attention towards focusing on solutions that can meet everyone's needs. Here, you might help the parties to restate vague or unclear requests and agreements. Unclear arrangements might otherwise soon stimulate a new conflict. One common source of conflict is when one person asks the other person to stop doing something, or not to do certain things. When you as a mediator hear the requests being expressed in a "no-form", you can help to reformulate these statements into what the person really wants.

"Whenever our objective is to get somebody to stop doing something, we lose power. If we really want to have power in creating change - whether it is personal change, changing another individual or changing society - we need to come from a consciousness of how the world can be better. We want people to see how their needs can be met at less cost."
Marshall Rosenberg[1]

To ensure that our wishes both are clear and do not sound like demands, we can find support in asking ourselves these two questions: "What do I want someone to do differently" and "What do I want their reasons to be when they do it?"

If we ask for something and discover that we want someone to do what we are asking for because it is their duty or because we say so, we can ask ourselves whether we really are prepared to pay the price. When people do something out of fear of being punished, the price is a loss of warmth

1 Rosenberg, Marshall (2005), *Speak Peace In A World Of Conflict, What You Say Next Will Change Your World.* Puddle Dancer Press.

and caring in the relationship.

It is much easier for people to find the will to contribute to others when they feel they can say "no" without defending themselves against locked, one-sided solutions.

Practice asking for what you want

Practice expressing clear requests as often as possible. Make them concrete and possible to say yes or no to. Be also aware of what happens when you or others do not express this type of request. If you maintain a consistent practice, you will sharpen your skills in being of help when two parties are trying to make a shared agreement during a mediation process.

Challenges

To be able to differentiate observing from judging

According to a traditional German story I once heard, there was once a man who could not find his ax. He suspected that the boy next door had stolen it. The boy walked like a thief, looked like a thief, and spoke like a thief. But one day the man found the ax when he was out in his forest. The next time the man met the boy, he looked, walked and talked like any other boy.

War is never far away when the culture we live in does not teach us to think in terms of needs, but instead teaches moral judgments, static language, "enemy" images and what is wrong with others. When we put labels on people and put people in boxes, we easily lose our compassion. It makes it harder for us to see the humanness in a person. When one fails to see the humanness in his fellow man, the step towards using violence is then much smaller.

We can, for example, study the horrible genocide in Rwanda. As mentioned earlier, the almost one million Tutsi people who were executed during a period of three months were called "cockroaches". During such heinous events, it becomes clear that people's "enemy" image of each other facilitates acts of violence.

To make concrete observations of what someone says or does, and to separate this from what we think about these things, is therefore an important step in NVC and in managing conflicts. An example of this is to separate the observation that someone is lying on the couch while the rest of the family is housecleaning, from the analysis that the person is lazy and irresponsible. If I communicate with someone on the basis of the interpretation: "You are lazy and irresponsible," as opposed to making the observation: "You are lying on the sofa while we others are cleaning", the communication will sound very different. What is more, it will probably produce very different results. People do not like to be placed in boxes, but want to be understood as to why they do what they do.

One way of clarifying to oneself whether something is an observation or an interpretation is to start from the point of view of a camcorder. A camcorder can capture what is happening, but it can not assess whether what it has captured is normal, abnormal, good, bad, inappropriate or appropriate. When we can restate exactly what we have seen someone do or heard someone say with the neutrality of a camcorder, we create an initial common platform for communication. Sometimes a conflict begins with a vague statement that leads to misunderstanding and upset feelings. Here, you as a mediator can help by clarifying ambiguities. It is difficult to reach out with information to people who are upset, if they haven't first been listened to on the level of feelings and needs.

All static thinking, that people "are" like this or that, can be put in different compartments, be assessed or categorized, can be transformed into language that more clearly describes processes.

If our view of human nature is based on the idea that people are constantly evolving, we can make observations that are rooted in specific situations and not confuse them with static analyses. A more process-oriented way of looking at people will make it easier for you in the role of mediator, especially if the people who participate in the mediation use static language and have strong "enemy" images of each other.

Static language vs process-oriented language

"You are lazy and irresponsible."
"But I am just resting."
"Yes, but you too must take responsibility and help like the rest of us."
"I am free to rest if I want to."

Our interpretations and analyses easily become self-fulfilling prophecies if we communicate these interpretations with the person we want to influence. If we want connection, but also want to influence the other person, we can instead communicate like this:

"When I see that you are lying on the couch and the rest of the family is cleaning, I get frustrated. I want us to help each other and I wonder how come you are lying there?"

"I'm just so very tired. I have not slept well the entire week."

"I understand that you need to rest and I also want you to get the rest you need. At the same time, I also want help, so I wonder if you would be willing to say yes to cleaning the kitchen before six o'clock because we are having guests?"

Enemy images

At one occasion it became clear to me how quickly an idea is created about how a person is and why she acts as she does. Here, I will use the word "enemy images" and by that I mean all static ideas and preconceived ideas about others.

A person asked if I wanted to help her find a Swedish publisher willing to translate from English to Swedish and publish her book. As a first step she was going to e-mail the English manuscript to me so that I could read it. I looked forward to this with great curiosity. Time passed and I did not hear from her. I sent several e-mails asking what had happened, but received no response. During this time there was a conflict in a network that we were both, in different ways, affected by. In some way, the feelings I had in relation to the network also "rubbed off" onto my thinking about my connection with her.

I began to analyze and interpret the situation in an attempt to understand what was going on. I began having somewhat paranoid thoughts about people talking about me behind my back, and thought that must be why she did not send me her manuscript. An assessment I made about her was therefore:

"She does not follow up on the things she says she wants to do, she is a coward and does not even dare to stand up for what she thinks."

A Helping Hand
Mediation with Nonviolent Communication

When we met some time later and got a chance to talk about the events, it became clear what had happened. While my "enemy" image of her had developed, she had been experiencing something similar herself. As it turned out, she had sent me exactly what we had agreed upon a few days after our first conversation, then waited eagerly for my comments. When she sent a subsequent e-mail and still did not get any response, a similar reaction started in her head. She became more and more certain that I had not liked her book and that I had not bothered to e-mail her. She was disappointed at first, since her need of support and trust were not met. As time went on, the growing bitterness turned into irritation and an analysis of me became something like this: "She is arrogant and does not care about others. She can't even stand up for her opinions, and doesn't even care enough to write back."

All of our messages had disappeared - probably into some spam filter. When this became clear, we were amazed at how quickly our inner fantasies had grown into "truths". This had made it harder and harder to reach out towards one another after each unanswered e-mail.

We could eventually laugh about it and rejoice in the lessons we had received. We also saw how this could have grown into a conflict between us because we had begun to see the other through our own interpretations.

It became clear to me that when I began to separate my interpretations about this person from what had actually happened (the observations), the chance of creating connection was much greater. This is one of several powerful lessons I have had when distinguishing interpretations from observations. The observation was: "We agreed that she would send me information and I have not received it".

One of the possible interpretations was: "She has not sent the information." I see this as an interpretation, because I could not know this for a fact. Another more charged interpretation which I made a bit later was: "She doesn't follow up on things she says she will do. She is a coward and doesn't even dare to say what she thinks."

Sometimes misunderstandings like what I have described go so far that a third party is needed to restore the broken connection. The pain generated by the "enemy" image itself may be so strong that listening to what the other person is really saying seems impossible. Even if one side provides details about what actually has occurred, it can completely miss the mark if the other side hasn't first been heard in their pain, frustration and disappointment.

If something has happened that has disrupted the connection, it is helpful if a mediation is carried out as soon as possible thereafter. If a long period of time has passed, the "enemy" image of either party can grow, and it can become more difficult to see the humanness in the other person or persons.

Keep in mind that opinions or interpretations expressed by the mediator are also difficult to handle for the parties. It creates more security if you as a mediator can really stick to your observations, feelings, needs and requests.

Observation or interpretation, depending on the point of view

1. One person says:
   "I always do whatever she asks for as soon as she asks for it"!

   The other person describes his/her point of view on the same situation:
   "She never does anything - until I ask her to"

   What has actually happened? Describe it in terms of observations, instead of by the interpretations used above.

2. One person says:
   "He is cold and doesn't care about other people's well-being"

   The other person says:
   "I am considerate, I never interfere in others' privacy"

   What has actually happened? Describe it in terms of observations instead of by the interpretations used above.

Conflicts lead to conflict

It makes things easier if we can summarize what has happened between two parties by calling it "a conflict". However, I have heard people have a strong reaction to the word conflict itself. There can, for example, exist strong taboos in a family or a working group against having conflicts. People then want to avoid calling anything a conflict. In tense situations, interpretations and analyses are often even more charged than usual.

When we say: "this is a conflict" we make an interpretation about what is going on between people or groups. Because the term conflict is often negatively charged, it is useful if you as mediator are clear about which observations you base this interpretation on. In other words, what you have seen or heard that you call a conflict.

The situation can improve greatly if you as a mediator notice a negative reaction to the word conflict. Someone might say: "I do not feel that we have a conflict, we just have a little different view on how the work is done".

If this occurs, you as a mediator might acknowledge what the person is saying by reformulating the interpretation into an observation of what has happened. When you would normally have said: "When you think of your conflict ...". You can instead say something like: "When you think about how you have talked about this during at least five staff meetings ..." or: "When you hear that you have different preferences about how things are carried out ...". Try to describe the situation as closely as possible, instead of taking a "shortcut" and calling it a conflict. You can of course also ask if anyone has anything against calling what happened a conflict, just to keep things simple.

There are several other words and expressions that people may have strong reactions towards. The most common ones are expressions that include diagnosis, analysis and labels on people.

Reflect on "Conflict"

- What does the word conflict mean to you?

- When do you start calling something a conflict, and when do you choose to call it something else? (Maybe you need to think of a specific situation to find clarity on this point.)

- Describe what happens in the language of observations; what you actually see and hear that you call a conflict.

- How would you describe your "conflict history"? How has conflict been part of your life?

Conflicts exist on the level of strategies - not on the level of needs

The more I have been involved in conflicts over the years, the more I've seen that what leads families to argue—what lead nations to war—the more I believe that most school children could resolve these conflicts. Marshall Rosenberg[1]

Being able to distinguish between needs and the way people try to meet their needs is an important distinction for the mediator to be clear about. When you can distinguish between these, you can help the parties to effectively find other ways to resolve conflicts rather than compromising or using methods based on "the winner takes all".

Since we all have the same needs, focusing on needs helps people to identify with each other. If we can see needs as something human in general and not tied to a specific person, time or place, it is easier to find solutions in a conflict situation. At times, when a solution is not found, it may be important to ask ourselves whether we really have everyone's needs "on the table".

When we are in the midst of a conflict, it is easy to focus on what we ourselves see as the problem. If we instead focus on what we need or what we dream of, it can open completely different doors.

It may be useful to remember that a conflict rarely or never occurs unless the people involved have strong interests, values or dreams. To be deeply involved in something makes us more willing to stand up for what we believe in and dream about. Here, conflicts can easily occur, especially when someone else is also passionate about something that seems to be in conflict with what we want. We can view these conflicts as an opportunity to learn new things and leave behind old ways of communicating that do not help us any longer.

To really pay attention to what people are dreaming about, are interested in, value and want to see happen, and then to be able to focus on this, is an important ingredient in your role as a mediator.

---

1 Rosenberg, Marshall (2008), *We Can Work it Out*. Puddle Dancer Press.

Empathy

In NVC the term "empathy" or to "listen with empathy," describes a specific way of approaching someone. To listen with empathy can be described as a respectful way of showing understanding towards what others are experiencing, without agreeing or feeling sorry for them. As a mediator, I try to be present with how someone is experiencing something, and listen with my whole being. I do not try to "fix" people or try to resolve their problems, but instead show that I am interested in understanding their situation and how it would be to "walk a mile in their shoes."

Empathy occurs when we no longer judge or have preconceived ideas about people, but instead really listen with an open heart to what they are feeling and needing. We are present with what is going on in them. Empathy can be communicated without words, but our words are a way of confirming that we really are trying to understand what is going on in the person. Supported by the principles in NVC, I listen for people's feelings and needs, because focusing on this tends to stimulate empathy. Weakened compassion for the other party is a common characteristic of conflicts. One of the most important tools we have available as a mediator is to listen with compassion to the pain and frustration expressed by the parties. When someone has experienced something painful, they usually experience relief when responded to with empathy. To be heard at depth tends to awaken their own compassion towards the other party. This leads to more ease in listening and in trying to understand in both parties.

When we choose something else than empathy

The following list consists of examples of some common ways we humans respond to each other. Depending on the context, they have various effects, but they are often counter-productive in mediation situations. Responding with empathy is often what makes the parties open up and talk about what they need. For example, one party in a conflict might say:

"I have just about had it with this relationship because it will never improve!"
An empathy guess could sound like this:
"Is it that you feel great despair because you yearn so much to experience cooperation and support in your relationship?"

It may be useful to learn to recognize other ways of responding to people and to consider how you act.

1. Advising: "I think you should . . . " "How come you didn't . . .?"
2. One-uping: "That's nothing; just wait until you hear what happened to me."
3. Educating: "This could turn into a very positive experience for you if you just . . . "
4. Consoling: "It wasn't your fault; you did the best you could."
5. Story-telling: "That reminds me of the time . . . "
6. Shutting down: "Cheer up. Don't feel so bad."
7. Sympathizing: "Oh, you poor thing . . . "
8. Interrogating: "When did this begin?"
9. Explaining: "I would have called but . . . "
10. Correcting: "That's not how it happened."

The difference between empathy and sympathy

If you as a mediator approach a party at a preparatory meeting with sympathy rather than with empathy, there is a risk that this will contribute to an amplified conflict. Therefore, it is important that you can distinguish between approaching someone with empathy and approaching someone with sympathy. When I listen with empathy, I try to understand how someone is experiencing things on the level of needs. I focus on being present with the person and paying attention to what he or she is feeling and needing. If I listen with sympathy, I am agreeing, pitying, or blaming someone else for the person's feelings. I might take over the conversation and begin to talk about similar events to show that I really understand the person. Unfortunately, this seldom leads to a greater understanding in the way I want.

At a preparatory meeting prior to a mediation connected to a juvenile crime, a young boy who had been beaten by another boy was asked what he wanted to get from the mediation:

"I just want to scream at him that he is a shitty bastard and beat the crap out of him."

His mother, who was also present with him, was horrified by this statement and immediately tried to get him to calm down. Rather than trying to calm the boy, the mediator responded with empathy to what the boy had said. She guessed that the boy wanted to be heard in the great anger and disappointment he felt:

"It sounds like you're really upset and want to let us know how this has been for you?"

He replied:

"Yeah, he's an idiot! He doesn't understand anything but fighting!"

The mediator chose to continue to hear him with empathy:

"So you're pissed off and it's important for you to get across just how painful this whole thing has been for you?"

This continued for a while until the boy calmed down and realized that he did not at all want to use violence because it would not make things any better. His mother thanked the mediator afterwards and told of earlier times when she had tried to get her son to calm down. Trying to calm him down had only caused them to drift further apart. She now understood that her way of relating had contributed to him rarely confiding in her any more. Her intention was, of course, to try to prevent him from doing things that he would later regret. However, his needs were not to seek advice or to be told to calm down.

Here is an example of how the dialogue could have sounded if the mediator had responded to the boy with sympathy in the same situation:

"I just want to scream at him that he is a shitty idiot and beat the crap out of him."

"I understand that you are angry, I would also be angry if I was treated that way."

"Yeah, they are all the same in that family. The only thing they understand is fighting. I'll show him that he is not the only who can use his fists."

"I fully understand that you do not want to be someone who people boss around. It must be a really tough situation."

"Yeah, damn right! He'll see what happens if he gets in my face!"

When you approach people with sympathy, they may indeed feel understood, but there is also a considerable risk that they may get "fired up". The enemy image they have of the other person can grow. Sympathy can therefore enhance the connection with the listener, but the price is a further decrease of connection with the other party.

We meet someone with sympathy by suggesting that the cause of the person's feelings is what another person has done.

As a result, the person might become convinced that the reason for her feelings is what the other person does. She then may experience even greater difficulties in seeing clearly what she needs. Furthermore, a feeling of powerlessness may make punishments seem very attractive from that position.

Advice instead of empathy

Here is another illustration of an attempt to approach the boy from the previous example. Rather than giving him empathy, the mediator gives him advice:

"I just want to scream at him that he is a shitty bastard and beat the crap out of him."

"Yes, but you must understand that the best thing for you right now is to let it go and to move on."

"Yes, that's easy to say for someone who has never been in the situation!"

"No, I haven't, but becoming aggressive will, of course, not be good for you."

"You've got no idea how you would react if you were in a situation like this!"

Giving advice is an attempt to help the person, but if it is not what a person wants just then, it creates more distance rather than giving any real help. Giving advice is often a way of managing one's own worry and insecurity about how to deal with a difficult situation and the strong reactions it stirs up.

As a mediator, it is important that you can decide whether it is helpful to switch from listening with empathy, to expressing honesty about what is going on in you. Rather than simply giving advice, you might express what is going on in you and what you want the person to do in order to help you meet your needs. You do this without judging, demanding or criticizing. The intention behind your honesty is to deepen the connection between one another and to try to meet more needs. It might sound like this:

"When I hear you say that you most of all want to beat him, I get scared. I have very little confidence that this way to deal with the situation will give you what you want. So, I wonder if you and I can come up with other ways to handle the situation?"

Reflecting back exactly what someone has said

In some situations, it is comforting for the parties to hear the mediator rephrase in detail what is being said. This can boost the trust that you, as a mediator, really are trying to understand what has happened. However, there are some things to watch out for when you reflect back what someone has said. If person A says:

"So I just have to overlook the fact that you have ignored all my previous attempts to cooperate and have trust that it will work this time?!"

Rephrasing this example by using the sentence below, risks giving the other party the feeling that you are taking sides or agreeing with things that are interpretations of what happened:

"So you want to get some understanding for the many times that she has ignored you?"

If you do this, it is not surprising if person B exclaims:

"But I have never ignored her attempts. It has just never been clear to me what she wanted. She has never..."

By not choosing to restate the interpretation "ignored", the relationship might have become even more tense and you could have one more thing to sort out. Instead, rephrase what you hear with a reference to what has happened, without using the previously expressed interpretations. If you want to reflect back without using the interpretation "ignore", you might say:

"Is it so that when you think about your past attempts to contribute to cooperation, it becomes clear to you how much you yearn to be able to have confidence that things get done? Would you like to have understanding about how much doubt you are feeling?"

Or:

"You want understanding for how much earlier experiences still affect you, especially when you think about what happened to you when you last called. Is that what you mean?"

Mixing feelings with thoughts

There are some words that may make a conflict difficult to manage. When we mix strong emotions with thinking that someone else is the cause of them, we make it even more difficult for others to hear us. It may, for example, be words such as "manipulated", "attacked" or "insulted".

If I say that I feel "manipulated", it is very easy to hear this as I am saying "you are manipulating" me. If I instead say that I feel "scared, because I have a need for trust" or "angry, because I have a need for respect", it tends to be a bit easier to hear. Here are some more words to be careful with for everyone who is part of a mediation, and especially for you as mediator.

abandoned	*cheated*	*interrupted*
abused	*coerced*	*intimidated*
attacked	*co-opted*	*let down*
betrayed	*cornered*	*manipulated*
boxed-in	*diminished*	*misunderstood*
bullied	*distrusted*	*neglected*

A Helping Hand
Mediation with Nonviolent Communication

overworked	*rejected*	*unseen*
patronized	*taken for granted*	*unsupported*
pressured	*threatened*	*unwanted*
provoked	*unappreciated*	*used*
put down	*unheard*	

Sort out your listening

You can simplify your listening by thinking that you are doing a general allocation of everything someone says into two categories: "thank you" or "please help me". We express a request for help (please help me), when our needs are not met. When our needs are met, we express joy about something we appreciate (thank you).

A simple first step for practicing our capacity to empathize is to listen for which of these two things a person is expressing. You can, for example, do this by selecting one person each day whom you listen to in this way. You can also select a specific time of day. For example, you may want to do this during lunch, and listen for "thank you" or "please help me" in what people are saying.

The ultimate solution

If we get the idea that there is an ultimate solution to a conflict, we risk missing something important. Instead of looking for the "right" solution or the "best" solution as a mediator, aim for reducing the distance between the two parties. Eventually, you are looking for a solution that meets needs, not the "right" solution. To demonstrate this, I want to share an example from when I was choosing wallpaper for an upstairs room in my home.

At first, it felt fun and inspiring. I browsed through lots of wallpaper catalogues, comparing colors, shapes and prices. After a while I began to feel more and more pressured and my joy shrunk for each new catalogue I looked at. Every time I thought I had found what I was looking for, a new idea or color combination showed up.

It began feeling like a burden, and I realized that it was not the wallpaper catalogues, but the way I looked at them that was the reason for my lack of joy. When I investigated my attitude a bit deeper, I realized that I was looking at the wallpapers thinking that I would find the best wallpaper, the one that was just right. To my relief, I found another way to approach the situation. Instead of asking myself what the "ultimate" wallpaper looked like, I focused on trying to answer the question of what mood I wanted in the room, what I would do there and what colors and shapes would support this. (Not the "best" support because then I easily would have slipped into the same thought-pattern as before.) I switched focus to what I wanted, needed and dreamed about. It then became much easier to choose and be happy with what I had chosen.

As a mediator, I often experience support just by reflecting upon this story at times when I constrain myself to the idea that a conflict must be resolved in a certain way. It has helped me to be more open towards changing my attitude and moving a step closer towards what is important for the parties in the conflict.

The price we pay for getting stuck defending one position

It is useful if you can help the people you are mediating between to not get stuck defending their own positions in a conflict. Helping them to let go of their preferred solutions to the conflict might be a major step forward in dealing with the conflict.

When someone defends his point of view, it can end up like the classic breakdown in negotiations that occurred between the United States and the Soviet Union concerning the ban on nuclear weapons. The parties were dealing with the question of how many inspections per year the United States and the Soviet Union would undertake on each other's territories. In order to investigate suspicious seismic records in the Soviet Union, the United States demanded at least ten inspections of nuclear missiles. The Soviet Union did not agree to more than three. Negotiations broke down, though no one had made it clear what was meant by "inspection" Did it mean ten inspections by one person or three inspections by fifty people? Would the inspection last one day or thirty days? If the parties had described their interests and wishes, they would have had a greater opportunity to reach a solution that could work for both of them.

If both parties had listened to exactly why they each wanted to get their proposal through, what interests and needs they were trying to meet, they would have found that the Soviet Union wanted to work in peace without being disturbed, thereby opting for fewer inspections. The United States, on the other hand, wanted maximum transparency, then to know that things were handled in a safe way. They could then have worked together to find a solution based on both a desire to work in peace and an insurance for maximum security.

The more you as a mediator can help the parties to see beyond the positions which they seem to get stuck in, the more chances are greater that they will find a satisfactory solution for all parties. In order for the parties to be willing to drop their positions, they need to feel confident that they will get understanding regarding what is important to them and that this will be considered in the conflict resolution.

How big is the cake?

Many people enter a mediation thinking that the possibilities for resolving the conflict are already clear. They believe that they understand where the concerns lie, what the problem is and so on. This attitude limits openness to new ways of dealing with the situation. It blocks the creativity that could support finding solutions that no one previously imagined.

As a mediator, it is important that you are open to the idea that there may be solutions to the conflict that no one has thought of before. If you approach a mediation process in this way, you can help by not getting stuck in a certain solution or that the situation can not be solved at all. If you do not see this clearly, there is a risk that you will affect the parties to become even more strongly opposed to each other.

A challenge might be someone approaching the mediation thinking that either "you get what you want or I get what I want". Relating to this situation with a "both/and", rather than "either/or", thought has helped me to keep myself open to events or solutions that no one could predict beforehand. This happens when the parties have reached the deeper connection that I have previously written about.

The following story serves to remind us of this:

Two sisters are fighting over an orange. Both are arguing as to why they should have it, it is their turn, the other one always gets her way and so on. When they finally agree, they decide to compromise and split the orange in two parts, taking half each. The first sister takes her half, peels it, throws away the peel and eats the fruit. The second sister, peels it, throws away the fruit and uses the peel for a cake she is baking.

If we approach a conflict with a "lack-of mentality" and a finished idea about what will happen, we are not open to new creative ways to resolve the conflict. An attitude that helps me when mediating a conflict is to think that there are always resources to meet people's needs, but not always in the way they first had wished for or imagined.

I once mediated between a man and a woman in a working group. For a long time, there had been a conflict between them that had affected the entire group in a significant way. Prior to the mediation, several people in the working group told me about past events that had led to the situation where, as soon as these two people participated in a conversation, everyone else was on edge, wondering when a quarrel would break out.

The working group felt that they had tried everything, prior to inviting me to mediate. During a few preparatory conversations, it became clear that they in fact had made several attempts to get these people to understand each other. Unfortunately, these attempts had been based on the idea that, in order to resolve the conflict, they had to persuade the two people to communicate more with each other. What they hadn't done was to find out what the needs and interests of these people were that were blocking connection between them. Instead, they had gotten stuck in the strategy that these two people must be helped to talk to each other.

When I focused on the needs of both parties during the mediation, it became clear that the woman had a need for peace and quiet. She had tasks that required concentration and wanted most of all to work in silence without being disturbed. The man however, had a need for support and fellowship because he had such tasks that were best solved by different people giving their views on them.

The actual mediation talk did not take long. We simply came up with a solution based on planning their work so that no one was directly dependent on communicating with the other in order to complete their tasks.

The man was able to get the support he needed from another co-worker in order to carry out his duties. This was a big contribution for the woman, creating the peace and quiet she sought in her work.

To everyone's surprise, even to their own surprise, the two "antagonists" joked with one another after the mediation. Their connection had become much more relaxed and open when they didn't feel forced to communicate with each other.

Two months later I met the working group for a follow-up. Several people in the working group said that they had been surprised at how much more relaxed and fun it had become at work. They had not been aware of how much energy the conflict had drained from everyone.

Compromising or shifting

When my father grew old and became ill, he had many difficulties communicating with my mother. For example, he wanted to continue driving a car despite having had several heart attacks, was quite confused and had not driven for a long time.

Once, after Mom and Dad had left after having visited us, Mom came back and asked for help. Dad had taken the driver's seat and was determined to drive the car. Mom refused to go with him. They argued loudly over which of them would have to give in.

I didn't have to listen for long to guess what mom's needs might be, so I asked:

"Mom, are you upset and worried because you want to make sure that neither you, Dad or anyone else gets hurt?"

After she had confirmed that this was so, I asked Dad to reflect back what he had heard Mom's needs to be. He said:

"She just wants to control me. She thinks she can decide for me and..."

Here, I interrupted him and said:

"I heard her a bit differently. I understood that she wants to be sure that nobody will get hurt. She wants to be safe. Do you want to try again?"

After some resistance, including an analysis of how Mom was and what she should support him in, he was finally able to restate what she was needing, in a way that she was satisfied with.

Then I tried to understand what my dad's needs were. I guessed that it was both a need for respect and to be understood in how much it meant to him to still be able to drive a car. He confirmed my guesses. I turned to Mom and asked her to tell what she had heard Dad's needs to be. She replied:

"But he is always so stubborn and inflexible and never listens..."

I interrupted her as well, telling her what needs I had heard Dad express. After a similar process of resistance, as with Dad previously, she reflected his needs in a way that worked for him.

I was also listening to myself with empathy from time to time when thoughts like: "How hard can it be?!" and "I give up, this isn't getting anywhere" sprung up. Sometimes, I found that I was taking sides with one of them, and then suddenly taking sides with the other. Because my heart was yearning to contribute to both these people, it was difficult for me to have hope when I heard how they were communicating with each other. I longed to see more care for both of them and felt both sadness and despair when I listened to how they were struggling (with something which I easily could think was really "trivial") to reach each other. It was so obvious that the way they communicated made it difficult for them to meet each other.

This whole process of listening to and reflecting back each other's needs, was valuable for both of them and reduced both the tempo and volume of the conversation. Also, both could stick to what they valued most, without it being at the expense of what the other wanted. We then settled for an agreement that might look like a compromise. Actually, it was an important shift in the dialogue; both were even contributing to fulfill each other's needs. Dad drove the car down our long driveway where no one could come to harm. Since Mom didn't want to ride in the car while Dad was driving, she walked that stretch instead. This enabled Dad to regain some of his self-respect while he could also contribute to Mom's need for safety.

If we hadn't done the necessary "preparatory work" of trying to understand each other, and were just trying to reach a compromise, there would have been a risk that one or both of them had experienced "giving up" something. My experience is that this is very common when making compromises. Compromises may be temporary and quickly resolve problems, but on the down side they create dissatisfaction in the relationship afterwards. In this situation, Dad got his need for respect met and Mom got her need for security met, without either of them having to give up something.

How they came to the solution was at least as important as the solution they came to. Mom told me afterwards that they had continued to talk in the car on the way home about what they would do about Dad's desire to drive a car and her concern about that. They could hear each other in a way they were not able to do before, and thereby were able to become closer to each other.

To hear each other's needs, and to really take in what others want, makes a difference because it helps us to trust that others wish us well. This trust allows us, in turn, to be more open towards also hearing the other person and to seek ways to meet everyone's needs.

When we really focus on everyone's needs, it helps us to feel trust. Ultimately, this is more satisfying than finding a compromise, because a compromise is not likely to meet everyone's needs fully in the end.

In my experience, if we move too quickly to strategies, we may find some compromises, but we won't have the same quality of resolution. If we thoroughly understand needs before moving to proposed solutions, we increase the likelihood that both parties will stay with the agreement. Marshall Rosenberg.[1]

Body language that matches the words

When I do a workshop in Nonviolent Communication and we twist and turn how things can be expressed in words to create more connection, there is often someone who exclaims:

"But most of our communication is, after all, through our body language, so why is this so important?".

I fully agree that we communicate largely through intonation, gestures, facial expressions and body movements. And since we do this, it becomes all the more important that we find words that go with what we have already communicated with our body language. To put into words the feelings that others have already imagined that we are experiencing, based on our facial expression, tone of voice and gestures, we can avoid double meanings. It makes it easier for people to understand what we mean. This means that I need to be willing to be honest about what is going on inside of me, which is sometimes a challenge.

---

1 Rosenberg, Marshall (2008), We can work it out. Puddle Dancer Press.

What you as a mediator communicate with your voice and tone may in some situations be very sensitive. Some language can, for example, be perceived as ironic, punitive or superior. It can stir up strong feelings and contribute to reluctance towards continuing the mediation. If either party expresses doubts about how you are expressing yourself, you can see it as a help and a reminder to connect with your intention to mediate.

When I have been with parties who have used facial expressions, gestures or other forms of body language which have been challenging for me, I have reminded myself of one of the basic principles behind NVC: "people do everything they do to try to meet their own needs". When I try to connect with the feelings and needs that may exist behind the body language, my discomfort usually subsides.

You can consciously make use of body language such as gestures, hand movements and eye movements during a mediation. When the heat is on, the parties may have an easier time recognizing a raised hand together with a STOP, than just hearing the word itself. You might remind the parties about your presence, for example, by putting a foot between them, or leaning forward in order to attract attention when needed.

Touch

Another thing to be clear about is what effect the mediator might have by touching someone during a mediation. Not only is touch perceived differently from person to person, touch can also be interpreted differently in different cultures. For example, if you gently touch the arm of the person who you want to hear honesty from, it can sometimes create safety and be perceived as if you really want to be supportive. However, the same touch can be experienced as if you are trying to calm down, hush, control or take sides with someone. Putting a hand on one party, for example, can be perceived as if you are taking sides.

Touch can also have a tremendously beautiful and calming effect. It can help to create trust and a longing for compassion and connection. Here, the same principle, as always, can be applied when it comes to mediation: focus on helping the parties deepen their connection and their ability to make decisions, and use touch if you see that it supports this purpose.

Chapter 6
The mediator's tool box

Tools used at a mediation

3. Interrupting

4. Emergency
   First Aid
   Empathy

2. Helping the
   parties to reflect
   back what they
   have heard

5. Self-Empathy
   and honest
   expression

1. Listening and
   translating

6. Tracking

1. The ability to listen with empathy and to translate what is said so that it has the potential of creating connection.

2. The ability to help people to listen to each other, "pulling them by the ear".

3. The ability to interrupt in a way that supports the dialogue.

4. Knowing how to give "Emergency First Aid-Empathy" when needed.

5. The ability to empathize with oneself and to express yourself when needed.

6. The ability to follow and keep track of what's going on.

The more the principles of NVC are integrated into a person's life, the easier it becomes to use them in a charged situation or conflict. This applies to situations where you are part of a conflict as well as situations where you are a third party.

This chapter contains a presentation of some concrete tools used in mediation with the help of NVC. In Chapter 7, there are exercises for integrating and practicing each of these tools. You might want to practice the tools separately at first, practicing each part individually and then as a whole. Go back and read the text for each tool in this chapter before doing the exercises. When you have sufficient knowledge about the various tools, use the tool that best suits the situation.

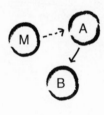

1. Listening, translating and rephrasing what is being expressed

If we thoroughly understand needs before moving to proposed solutions, we increase the likelihood that both parties will stay with the agreement.
Marshall Rosenberg[1]

As a mediator, it is important to listen for the observations, feelings, needs and requests expressed by each person. This means that the mediator tries to hear these parts, even when they are expressed in terms of insults, demands and judgments. We listen for these parts because it is easier to establish connection with the human being behind the words when we listen in this way.

When we listen to other people's needs, interests, dreams and requests, it also becomes clear that just because we understand what drives a person, it does not mean that we agree with them. The realization that we don't need to agree with someone, though we understand their point of view, usually makes it easier for the parties to listen to each other. This, because it increases their confidence that it is not taken as "I am agreeing with" something.

When you use what in NVC is known as "listening with empathy", you are translating what someone is saying to what they are feeling and needing when they express themselves. As a mediator, I gain tremendous benefit in

1 Rosenberg, Marshall (2008), We can work it out. Puddle Dancer Press.

A Helping Hand
Mediation with Nonviolent Communication

being able to focus my listening in this way, since it leads me directly to the core of the conflict. To be heard with empathy and to be understood in depth is what most people who are involved in a conflict long for.

As each party is expressing themselves, you can rephrase what was said, but in the form of observations (rather than interpretations), feelings (rather than thoughts) and needs and requests (rather than demands). This is usually called paraphrasing and is expressed as a guess because you, of course, never can know for certain what is going on inside another human being. You make the guess to really ensure that you have sensed what the person wants you to hear. In this way he or she receives confirmation that you have heard what was said. They then may correct us if we have heard them incorrectly. Misunderstandings are therefore minimized.

For example, you might guess:

"Have I understood you correctly that what you most of all long for is ...?"

Or,

"So you mean that what you are really interested in is ...?

Or,

"Is it so that what you are needing is ...?

To separate the needs from the strategies used to meet these needs is an important part of dealing with conflicts. If the parties are clear about their own and each other's needs and requests, it is easier to find solutions that work for everyone. When someone is absolutely convinced that a conflict must be resolved in a certain way, it is difficult for him or her to bring in the other's reality, and it becomes a challenge to find a way to satisfy everyone's needs.

When I have mediated in situations where someone is holding on tightly to their position, there has been a lot of fear behind the resistance towards alternative solutions. The parties have been afraid that their needs and interests won't be seen as important and therefore won't be taken into consideration if they give in.

When people struggle to get in touch with their needs, you can help by guessing what you think the person is feeling and needing. In a conflict, I believe that it is very helpful to get a confirmation that people understand what is going on inside of me by rephrasing what they have heard that

I feel. Initially, hearing someone putting words to one's feelings can feel a bit naked and frightening, but after a while it contributes to a greater sense of security and confidence.

In sensitive situations, it is important to be mindful of what words we choose. For example, words such as "vulnerable" or "sad" sometimes provide a clearer description of what is going on inside a person, than the word "sorry" does.

There might be strong taboos about feeling, expressing and talking about feelings in some settings. As a mediator, you can contribute to ease and safety by avoiding putting the feelings into words. Rather you might want to focus more on expressing the needs you are hearing the parties express. Remember that the purpose is not to follow a certain form, but to create connection between the parties so that they can find ways to reach an agreement through that connection.

To understand what someone feels contributes to a deeper sense of connection, so always pay attention to what you think the parties are feeling, even if you don't rephrase these feelings in words. After a while, the atmosphere in the conversation might change, the tension might let go and words describing what the parties may feel might be both welcomed and create clarity. As a mediator, you can always just focus on what the parties are feeling, without putting words to them, thereby making it easier for you to put yourself in their shoes.

At the beginning of a mediation, especially if it is emotionally charged, it may be helpful to use just one or two words to describe the needs of the involved people. For example, it might sound like this:

"You really want to be understood?"

Or,

"Safety is what is most important to you?"

Once the parties have come a bit closer to one another, it is easier for them to hear longer sentences; you can reflect what you hear using more words. Be aware that if you use many words to describe a need, it may sound as if you're referring to a strategy to meet the need, instead of the actual need itself. If the words you say don't help the parties hear each other's needs, it may, rather than deepening the connection, contribute to freezing it at a certain level.

When I am talking about needs, I am referring to universal driving forces shared by all people. Strategies, by contrast, are what we do to fulfill needs. A need is general and not tied to any particular individual doing something in order to fulfill that need. Here is an example where the needs are for support and understanding, while the guess more reflects the strategy that can meet these needs:

"Are you saying that you need B to understand your situation and change how he acts in these situations?"

To clearly express universal human needs you could guess something like this instead:

"Are you saying that you want understanding for the challenges that this has created in your life?"

The risk that this is perceived as criticism or a demand is minimized in the second example because the need to be understood is not tied to a certain strategy. We have separated the important need to be understood from the strategy, which involves one specific person to provide the understanding. This makes it easier to manage the conflict, because it opens up other ways of fulfilling needs rather than just the single strategy of only one person showing understanding.

2. "Pulling someone by the ear" – helping the parties to understand each other

Helping parties better understand each other's reality is another great task for you as a mediator. Particularly in the beginning, effort is required from you in order for this to happen. You are focusing on everyone's needs being expressed and heard, by, for instance, asking both parties to rephrase what they have heard the other party needs. This shows that you are focusing on trying to meet everyone's needs and on what you think will contribute towards the solution to the conflict. At a planned, or formal mediation, you can explain this approach in advance.

When person B has rephrased the needs that person A has expressed, we shift towards paying attention to what person B needs. The willingness to reflect back the needs of the other party is an important step in moving the conversation forward. It is important to remember that even if the parties feel heard by you, it is essential that they also hear each other. Mediation is both about feeling heard by the other and taking in the reality of the other.

To help the parties hear each other, use every opportunity to repeat words that draw attention to needs. In this way, you help them see what both sides need so that they will be able to deal with the conflict in an effective way.

When person A has confirmed that she feels understood by you as mediator, ask person B to reflect back what he has heard person A say. To hear person B reflect back what he has understood that person A needs, helps to build trust and understanding between them. You may ask person B something like:

"Do you want to tell A what you hear is important to her?"

Or
"Do you want to tell A what she needs?"

Or
"Do you want to reflect back what needs you hear that A is longing to have met in your relationship?"

In a conflict, this is a big challenge for person B. Since we easily hear what people whom we are in conflict with say as criticism, demands or evaluations, a normal response might be:

"But I've already done all that."

Or
"She / he is always so demanding."

Avoid saying "no, that is not what she said", or "you got it wrong" or something that the other person can experience as a correction. In this situation, you can instead clarify what has been said by saying something like:

OK, "I heard it slightly differently. I heard A say that what is really important for her is ... It's not about agreeing or disagreeing, it's just about reflecting back what you have heard that she longs for. Would you give it a try?"

To fully hear the other person is difficult when you are in the middle of a conflict. So even if the reflecting back seems superficial, it is an important step in creating understanding for the other party. If either party has great resistance towards even reflecting back some of what they heard the other saying, it may help them to hear something like:

"I guess it still hurts you to think about what has happened. Nevertheless, I encourage you to try to take in the other's experience and what is important for him. Are you willing to try to reflect back what you have heard that he longs for?

In a charged situation, the listener often hears what is said as criticism or demands. Instead of concentrating on listening and rephrasing what the other person has said, they are thinking of how to defend themselves when they get a chance to say something. They might need lots of support to understand that even if they reflect what the other has said, they have not agreed with any opinion or action.

3. To interrupt

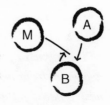

Many of us find it challenging to interrupt people who are talking. The longer we wait, the harder it becomes to interrupt with respect.

Our resistance usually comes from the idea that it is not polite or "correct" to interrupt. If you are afraid of getting on bad terms with someone, or worried about not being liked, there is a further challenge because in some cultures it is considered impolite and not very respectful to interrupt. In these situations, it is helpful to remind yourself that the purpose of interrupting is to create connection between the parties. As mediator you do this, not to take center stage yourself, but to protect the parties, to avoid "collisions" which may hurt one or both parties. Therefore, interrupt as soon as you think:

- *What is being said is likely to worsen an already tense situation*
- *What is being said can create distance, rather than generate dialogue*
- *Something is being expressed in such a way that it harms the connection between the parties*
- *Someone interrupts when you are listening to the other party and you want to continue listening to him or her*

- That which is being expressed is more than you think the other person can take in at that moment

To say that someone is "interrupting" is to make an interpretation of what someone is doing, a clear observation might be; she began talking while the other person was talking. If you see this clearly, and your intention is really to help the parties understand and connect with one another, it is easier to interrupt. You are simply aware that you want to contribute to dialogue and you are not fixed on whether it is good or bad to interrupt. The more emotionally challenging that people experience the mediation, the more important it becomes for you to show that you can handle the situation when things get stirred up. This gives the parties more of the security they need to dare to be more honest, or to listen to the other person. If the intensity increases so that neither you nor the parties are heard, you can interrupt by raising your voice. You can yell:
"STOP!"

and say:

"I am guessing it will be easier to understand each other if we sloooow doooown the proooocess. Would everyone be quiet for a while and get in touch with what is going on within you?"

When it is said slowly, it acts as a reminder that it can make a big difference to slow down the tempo when we want to create connection. If it raises serious reactions when you interrupt, you can move to the next tool in the toolbox, first aid-empathy.

During planned mediation talks (formal mediation), it is important to interrupt when someone is deviating from what you have agreed upon before the talk. If this happens, refocus directly on the approach which you have agreed upon. If you do not interrupt in this situation, it leads to insecurity and uncertainty about what the "ground rules" for everyone involved are. When you interrupt, you are demonstrating your belief that common agreements are valuable. This contributes to an increased level of security and also increases the parties' motivation to keep to what they have already said yes to themselves.

A Helping Hand
Mediation with Nonviolent Communication

4. First aid-empathy

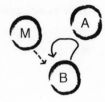

When the mediator is engaged in trying to understand person A, what A is saying can fuel more feelings in person B than he or she can bear to sit with in silence. If person B expresses these feelings before you have clarity about what person A wanted to say, you interrupt to protect the dialogue and ask him or her to wait. Person B's feelings can be so strong that you need to give him what in this section is called first aid-empathy. After having made empathy guesses about what is going on within him or her, you can also assure the person that you want to hear more as soon as it is clear to you what person A wanted to express. It is often the worry about not being heard or understood, that leads to one party refraining from fully listening to the other.

Make the empathy guess as brief as possible so that you do not lose connection with person A during this time. This is where the parable first aid-empathy, comes from. It is like putting a temporary tourniquet on a wound in order to find time to attend to other injuries so that no one bleeds to death.

How it sounds, of course, depends on the situation. For example:

"I guess you want to be sure that you will also be heard?"

(Moment of silence)

"I can only listen to one at a time and I want to get back to you. I wonder if you want to wait a while and instead continue listening to what A wants to say?"

Or

"Do you feel uneasy when you hear what is being said because you want to receive understanding for why you did what you did?"

(Moment of silence)

"I really want to hear you too and I only want to finish listening to what A says so that it is clear to me what she needs."

When you worry about something going on within a person and that he or she is no longer listening, showing that you are willing to hear his or her feelings (perhaps unexpressed) with empathy helps the person to deal with his or her strong emotions. Do it as quickly as possible, and then return to finishing listening to person A. It may sound like this:

"When I see your body language and facial expressions, I would guess that this is extremely painful for you. As soon as it is clear to me what A was just saying right now, I would very much like to hear what you want to say."

Anyone who is treated in this way usually hears it as a much-needed assurance that he or she will soon get a chance to express his or her view of the situation. You let the person know that you want to hear what they have to say, and also that you can only hear one person at a time. In tense situations this provides the sought after confidence and sufficient security to be able to continue the dialogue.

If one party is expressing evaluations about the other, there is of course a greater risk that it will be a challenge for the other party to continue being quiet and to listen. Listening to evaluations about oneself often leads to anger. Deal with the anger by saying for example:

"I suspect that it is enormously difficult for you to hear this. At the same time, I really want to continue this process so that we can get back to you as quickly as possible and hear you fully. Are you willing to wait a while longer?"

If the person still is not willing to move forward, you can get together and determine if you want to change the approach.

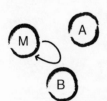

5. Self-Empathy - to empathize with oneself

As long as you are focused on hearing both parties, you are helping them to create conditions for connecting with each other. You will probably not be so useful if your attention is on:

- Evaluating yourself or the parties in terms of right/wrong, good/ bad etc,

- Blaming yourself or the parties,

- Putting labels on yourself or the parties,

- Moralizing and finding faults with yourself or the parties,

- Or comparing yourself with them.

When I listen to myself with empathy I do it in almost the same way as when I listen to another person. First and foremost, I acknowledge for myself what evaluations or demands I have of myself or of someone else. When I have done that, I focus on what needs I hear behind this and what I am feeling. Generally one can say that negative labels indicate that one's needs are not being met.

Because it seldom works to "push away" strong enemy images and self-criticism, your ability to quickly capture these thoughts and reformulate them into feelings and needs will be very useful.

Once you have done this, it might be possible for you to put your needs "on the shelf" for a while and concentrate on the mediation again. Proceed with the mediation as soon as you are confident that your evaluations of yourself or the parties don't lie in the way of your ability to mediate.

Reminding yourself of why you want to mediate can also help you to focus on both sides again.

Don't forget that you may also choose to express what is going on in you, if you sense it would add to the situation. When the mediator expresses his or her own observations, feelings and needs, it often contributes to the conversation. You become a role model for how things can be expressed, even though it is challenging to talk about it. On the other hand, it will be confusing and counterproductive if you express interpretations, evaluations, analyses, criticism or demands. If you are unable to get in touch with the needs behind your evaluations on your own, you can take a break. Use the break to get in touch with what is going on in you, either alone or with the help of someone else. You may only have brief periods of time for self-empathy during a mediation, so this means making your self-empathy crisp and effective. Use the exercises in the next chapter often, and practice, practice, practice.

> *We use NVC to evaluate ourselves in ways that engender growth rather than self-hatred.*
> Marshall Rosenberg[1]

---

1. Rosenberg, Marshall (2003), Nonviolent Communication: A Language of Life. Puddle Dancer Press.

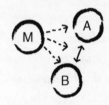

6. Tracking - to follow what is going on

A metaphor that may help you better understand your role as mediator is to see yourself as a traffic policeman directing traffic.

For example, you can ask someone to be quiet for a moment in order to let someone else move forward and avoid collisions. You can determine when it is time to interrupt, to help someone to hear what the person who is expressing himself or herself really wants to say.

As a mediator, you are helping to create a fabric where all threads contribute to a stronger connection between the parties. The threads are woven together into a common fabric instead of two separate ones, enabling the parties to understand how their actions are each affecting the other party. You will help them to weave the threads together by translating things that are difficult to hear. You show them how they can hear each other's needs and you interrupt when you see that a thread is fragile, on the verge of breaking.

You may also be involved in controlling the conversation, for example, by selecting who begins talking first. You might turn towards the person you think will have the most difficulties in hearing the other before he or she feels heard and understood (see more in the section "Who starts" in Chapter 8). Keep track of when the parties may be ready to go for solutions, as the connection on a need level has become stable.

As the process continues, keep track of whose needs are "on the table" and what will happen next. It is important to approach mediation with the attitude that no one can know for sure what the next step is, and to be open to quick changes in the dialogue.

An exciting and effective way to practice tracking whose needs are on the table, is by having a dialogue while an active four-year old is in the room! The dialogue will be repeatedly interrupted. Here, it is a challenge to quickly pick up the thread of what the dialogue had been focusing on at the moment it was interrupted, and to continue the dialogue until the next interruption.

A Helping Hand
Mediation with Nonviolent Communication

Cycles

We have now gone through the various tools that will be needed during most mediation talks. In order to more easily understand how the tools work together and create a whole, it may be helpful to think of mediation as a series of cycles.

Cycle 1: Person A expresses what he or she is needing, Person B reflects back the needs he or she has heard being expressed, with or without the help of the mediator.
The mediator asks person A if this is how he or she wanted to be understood and if so, turns to B in order to hear what is going on within him or her.

Cycle 2: Person B expresses himself, person A reflects back either with or without the mediator's help ... and so on.

Cycle 3: Person A ... (same as in cycle 1). When both parties' needs are clear, which sometimes involves many cycles, it is time to find together solutions based on the needs that have been expressed. Remember that these are guidelines of how a mediation can work and not rules on what is should look like. Be prepared to focus on what seems to help the parties create connection, independent of in what order things are said, or if it goes against the way you are used to working.

Problem-solving or reconciliation

"Is this mediation about solving a particular problem or is it about reconciliation and a deeper connection in a relationship?"

The difference between a mediation to support reconciliation and a mediation to handle a specific situation is sometimes vague. Mediation often involves a mix between problem-solving and relationship issues.

A mediation can begin with a conflict around a specific problem. After a while it might become clear that the situation calls for both reconciliation and healing deep wounds in the connection. When the tension around the original problem is gone, one or both parties may start talking about their longing for a different quality of connection between each other. If this happens, I suggest that you say something about what you hear; that you now have partly shifted focus.

Reconciliation

When it comes to reconciliation, there is not always a specific conflict or a clear problem to start from. If the mediation is about reconciliation, you focus on repairing and deepening the connection between the parties. This means, for example, that you choose to listen to each person a little bit longer each time before you move towards hearing the other person. By doing this, you get a chance to go deeper and find the core of the conflict.

Problem-solving mediation

During mediation around a specific question or difficulty, you approach the parties at the level needed in order to get clarity about everyone's needs. If you are working with a specific conflict, stay just long enough with these needs to complete a cycle, before switching over to the other person. Here, you don't focus as much on repairing the connection as in reconciliation. The needs and interests at stake in this particular question are highlighted, even if it is clear that there are other things going on. Problem-solving mediation primarily focuses on creating a deep enough connection between the parties in order to find a solution to the current problem.

Educate or mediate

As a mediator, it is important to be clear about whether your goal is to teach people something about communication that could make a difference for them in the long run, or if you just want to facilitate connection right now by "lending your ability to listen".

Mediation is, in many cases, about finding effective ways to deal with very specific issues or problems. However, the mediation process is also an opportunity for learning. People build communication skills through a combination of imitating others and trying things out for themselves. This means that the mediator becomes an important role model for constructive communication. You have many opportunities to affect the parties' way of communicating and managing a conflict inspired by the way you express yourself. For example:

- Giving a taste of how they can express feelings and needs - rather than criticism, threats or demands.

- Showing how they can listen to someone who has a different opinion than themselves and how they can hear that person's needs - rather than hearing criticism.

- Demonstrating how you can show an interest in how your choices affect others - instead of arguing and creating resistance.

- Demonstrating the advantages of not getting stuck on one exact solution – but rather being open to other solutions.

- Clarifying how you can show that you are willing to take in another person's reality – as opposed to sticking to your own way of seeing things regardless of what is happening.

Whether or not the parties are open to learning something new depends on at what stage of the conflict the mediation conversation is carried out. People who are upset and frustrated are rarely open to learning something new just then. Usually, the most important thing for people in these situations is to be heard and understood. They seldom want to receive advice or teachings about how they can express themselves differently just then.

Therefore, make sure that you clearly express when you want to move from mediation to education. For example, begin by saying:

"I'm worried that what you say will not be very easy for him to hear. Do you want to hear how you could say it instead?"

Another situation where teaching about a specific thing can contribute to the mediation process is when a person doesn't want to reflect back the needs they have heard the other person express. You can clarify the purpose of paraphrasing by saying:

"I'm asking you to reflect back what you have heard him say because I want a confirmation that what he needs and is interested in is clear. It doesn't mean that you have agreed with him or said yes to anything. So when you've heard this, I wonder if you are willing to reflect back what needs you heard him express?"

If you think that the parties are communicating in a wrong way, that you know better, or that this conflict must be resolved in a certain way, it is probably more constructive to take a break and get clear about what is going on in yourself, rather than to try to teach the parties you are mediating between. It is easier for others to be inspired when you imagine that you aren't in possession of any "right" way of dealing with the conflict.

Summary of the mediators' role

Listening - contributing to connection between the parties.

Translating – contributing to clarity and connection.

Letting the parties find their own solutions.

Supporting the parties with creation of solutions.

Chapter 7

Practise practise practise

Preparing to mediate

Being clear about what motivates your desire to mediate is of enormous value. With that clarity it will be much easier for you to really listen to both parties. The clearer you are about your own purpose in mediating, the more you can influence the dialogue to move into the direction that will serve both parties best, and your intervention will be most useful. If you are not clear about your intentions, it is harder to make conscious choices about how to handle different situations.

One way to become more aware of your own motivation is to ask yourself if you could accept that a mediation could fail to lead to both parties coming to an agreement; that the conflict remains unresolved. How do you feel imagining that - worried, afraid or annoyed? Do you feel hopelessness or resignation? Are your feelings centered around your desire to live in a world where there is a certain degree of harmony and caring about other people? Or is it about your longing to experience being able to safely express what you stand for, without the fear of relationships falling apart?

For example, if your longing for harmony is what drives your motivation to mediate, you could remind yourself that this need may not be met during the mediation itself. Perhaps the parties will be loud or threatening. It can be helpful to remind yourself that the need for harmony can perhaps be met after the mediation rather than during it. If you are aware of what is driving you, you will be helped to fully listen to all the involved parties, even if what they are saying is threatening what you desire.

Pitfalls and benefits

If we are aware of different needs we ourselves want to meet by mediating, it will be likely that we will act in a way that serves the handling of the conflict, and we can more easily avoid potential pitfalls. Below you will find some examples of pitfalls and benefits related to different needs and driving forces.

Harmony

If harmony is one of your main motivations, and during a mediation people scream louder and louder at one another, calling each other uglier and uglier names, perhaps you, often subconsciously, will interfere and attempt to calm the situation down. This means that you run a risk of preventing "all the cards being laid on the table", making it more difficult to find a solution that satisfies all parties.

Once you are aware that harmony is an important need for you, it could be easier to have this need unmet for a while, as you can take care of it at a later time. Having a more conscious relationship with that need can help you to better handle situations where strong feelings are being expressed and the surroundings do not support your own harmony.

Being aware of this particular need may increase your understanding that some parties may hesitate to be completely open because of a concern about disturbing harmony in the relationship.

Community

If valuing community is what drives you to mediate and the people in the conflict threaten to divorce, move apart, leave their job, and so on, you might be tempted to quickly find solutions that you think will get them together. If you are one step ahead of the parties in a conflict and are focusing on finding solutions before they are ready for them, your ability to fully listen to what they really need to be heard will be reduced.

One strength connected to being aware of your need for community is that it can enhance your willingness and ability to really consider the different needs of all parties when you are mediating.

Efficiency

Sometimes a mediation session can stretch far beyond the planned time. It may seem inefficient to dedicate so much time to allowing everyone to express themselves and to really listen to each other, instead of focusing on finding a solution.

Remind yourself that mediation is often primarily about re-creating trust and respect between the parties. When trust and mutual respect exist, the solution will usually come more or less automatically. If, as the third party, it is efficiency we strive for, it is easy to experience the many expressions of feelings as obstacles rather than something that contributes to developing a deeper contact between the parties and ultimately making handling the conflict easier.

One strength of being aware of this need and distinguishing it from various strategies is that it can help you focus on what really makes a difference. It can help you refrain from focusing on what leads to a quick solution that might not hold in the long run.

Contribution

Wanting to meet your need to contribute can be a valuable starting point to mediate from. It can help you to focus on what really contributes, instead of being tempted to solve the conflict for those you mediate between. Don't get caught in the idea that reconciliation has to happen in a specific way.

A major pitfall concerning the need to contribute is if you confuse the need to contribute with the strategy to contribute. If you are aware of the difference, you can be satisfied with what you have contributed, even if the mediation takes a different course than you hoped for.

To be seen

The pitfalls lying within this need are similar to those described under the need to contribute. If you are unaware of how important it is for you to be seen, you could, for example, want to "buy love". This can show itself in a number of ways: perhaps pay unequal attention to both parties, if one seems to pay more attention to you than the other. You may jump to a solution before it is time to focus on solutions. You may take up more space than required. You perhaps use fancy explanations or uncommon words to explain what is happening.

A strength here is being reminded of how important it is for humans to be seen and heard. You will therefore make sure that all of the participating parties in the mediation are listened to.

Autonomy and freedom

One of the obstacles that often exists when handling conflicts efficiently is threats or language that can narrow our sense of free choice. At a mediation where the parties are asked to express their needs, it is common that they formulate themselves by expressing what they think the other party should or must do. If your need for autonomy comes up in your role as mediator, a pitfall could be the temptation to argue when you hear someone making demands. You might be tempted to try to "prove" that we are all free to act the way we want. This can be an obstacle towards creating contact and can cause one or both parties to find it more difficult to have a sense of being heard and understood.

Having identified this need, it will remind you how much free choice means to people. It can help you to see all demands that can sneak in between the parties. It can also help you decide whether you want to continue mediating out of free choice, and not because you think it is your duty to be supportive.

Be clear about your purpose in mediating

To be efficient as a mediator it is a huge advantage if you understand which of your own needs you are trying to meet during the mediation process. Being aware of what is motivating you can help you to pay attention to any "pitfalls" that may exist. When you are clear about your own motives, you can make more conscious choices on how to act, even if your own needs are not met during the course of the mediation itself.

Write down which of your needs you want to have met after (or during) the mediation. See preceding pages to gain more clarity about the needs. Some examples of needs could be:

- Harmony

- Efficiency

- Community

- To contribute

- Respect

- To be seen

- Autonomy and freedom

- Interdependence

- Hope

- Meaning

- Love

If it is difficult for you to recognize your own intentions with only the help of words describing needs, you can finish the sentences below.

From these you can get some idea about what needs you want to meet by mediating.

If I were a mediator I couldn't bear that...

The worst thing that could happen when I'm mediating is....

When I'm mediating I hate to....

My dream about being a mediator is...

The perfect mediator always ...

A sign that I'm not good enough as a mediator is that...

If I can't manage to handle this conflict then...

Something that is really important for me is...

If I could choose, people would always...

The perfect mediation situation...

Another way to track your motivation in mediating is to reflect on how you want to feel after a mediation process. Read through what you have written and see if any needs catch your attention. You can also use the list of needs at the end of the book to find more words that may better describe your incentive to mediate. Come up with at least three other ways to satisfy these needs other than through mediation. This can contribute to your connection with the choices you have and make it a little easier for you to gain clarity over what you value when acting as a mediator.

Translating expressions that can get in the way of connection

Being able to hear the human needs behind what is said is one of the abilities that make us effective in mediating. This ability helps me meet those I am mediating between with empathy. It gives my role as a third party great power. My compassion awakens and is kept alive in keeping with my ability to hear the life-serving core in whatever is being said.

This can of course be a challenge, as most people involved in a conflict do not express their needs directly. Often people have already tried to solve misunderstandings and disagreements before they decide to bring in a third party. Most things have already been said, but in a way that has created distance rather than connection. In many cases the greatest challenge for the mediator is that strong emotions are expressed in a way which makes it hard for the other party to hear the intention behind them. Here the mediator's ability to rephrase what is being said is of great value. However, it is important to do so in a way that unites and contributes to compassion.

To be able to do this, most of us need a lot of training in listening and "translating". The mediator translates labels, demands and judgements into needs. Since most who are involved in a conflict are unable to directly express what they need, the mediator's ability to translate will often be utilized. This is very supportive to the parties.

Practicing on hypothetical situations is one way to enhance our ability to listen for what is important to creating connection. The following are some exercises where the mediation is broken down into different parts. You can practice each part separately before putting them together in a complete mediation. Like a football player who practices a particularly difficult kick before taking it into a game, you can work on what you find most challenging.

Some examples of what the mediator translates

Labels and judgments

"He's lazy and never does anything around the home", can be translated into:
"Are you longing for more relaxation and rest?"

Demands

"She has to learn that there some things you just have to do!"

Can be translated into:
"Are you worried and want to protect her so that she has an easier life?"

Threats

"If he doesn't start paying, I'll show him what happens to those who don't keep their promises to me!"

Even threats can be translated into needs, interests and dreams:
"It sounds as if you're extremely concerned because you have a need for support and want to be sure you will get it, is that so?"

Language that denies responsibility or freedom to choose

"I didn't have a choice, I was forced to do that because my boss told me I had to. "

This could be translated to make it clear where the responsibility lies, and in such a way that is easier for the other part to hear:

"Are you feeling worried and would like some understanding for what a tight situation you were in?"

Language that is built on "right and wrong" thinking

The mediator notices expressions that indicate that one person feels he is right and the other person is wrong.

"It is wrong not to think of others." Can be translated into something that is easier for the other person to hear, such as:

"Are you distressed about what has happened because it reminds you of how much you value that we show care for each other?

Blaming others

"She made me so sad when she broke our agreement."

By connecting all feelings a person expresses to his or her own needs, there is less risk of anyone interpreting what is being said as a demand, threat or blame distribution. When people hear demands they will either revolt or accept them. That is why the above could be translated into:

"Are you sad because it is important for you to be able to trust in agreements that are made?"

Translating what is being expressed so that it contributes to connection

The exercises below are aimed at helping you to improve your ability to translate challenging messages. The first step is to detect the things that the parties involved in a conflict are saying that you think are contributing to their inability to solve the conflict. The next step is to translate these things into expressions that have a greater potential to contribute to a connection being made.

The exercises can be carried out in a written format or by role-playing in small groups the people having the conversation.

Part 1: Translating what you as a mediator experience as a challenge when hearing what the parties are saying to each other

Write down what you would experience as challenging to hear during a mediation where you are the third party. Here are some examples of what could be a challenge for a mediator to hear during a mediation situation.

1. *"She just can't do this to us!"*

2. *"Now you do as I tell you!"*

3. *"He must learn not to be such an egoist!"*

Fill in the blanks with your own examples:

4. *He/she is _____(for example: abnormal, lazy, not caring enough)."*

5. *"He/she should _____(demands or expectations)"*

6. *"If you/he/she doesn't _____then _____(threat)."*

7. *"It's not right that/it's wrong that_____"*

8. Something else: "_____"

Guess the feelings and needs behind each of the examples. Translate both the finished suggestions and your own examples by asking yourself: What could the person saying this be feeling? Maybe it could be

_____?

What could the person saying this need? Maybe _____

_____?

Try translating:
"She just can't do this to us!"

Feeling: perhaps the person feels worried or scared?
Need: maybe the person is longing for care and connection?

For each of the sentences write down what you can say in order to help the person to connect with his or her own feelings and needs. In the example above it may sound like:
"Is it that you would like to have more understanding about how worried you feel? And is it so that you also want some understanding for how you long for more care towards yourself and the rest of the family?

Part 2: Translating what you as a mediator experience as a challenge to hear what the parties are saying

Write down something one of the parties could say to you which would be challenging to hear during a mediation. Some examples of this could be:

1. Let me finish what I have to say!"

2. *"It sounds like you don't know what you're doing, have you done this before?"*

3. *"It seems you've already decided who should be punished for this. You're on her side!"*

Write down your own examples of what you would find challenging to handle:

4. You are _____ (labels, judgments, analyses)

5. *You have to _____ (expectations and demands)*

6. If you don't _____ (threat),

I will_____.

7. "It's not right that/it's wrong that _____"

8. Something else: "_____"

Guess what feelings and needs are behind each of the above statements. Translate both the given examples and your own examples by asking yourself what the person who says that might feel.

For example:
1. "Let me finish what I have to say!"

What might this person be feeling?
Feeling: The person is probably annoyed?

What need could be behind what is being said?
Need: Maybe the person has a need of respect and to be heard?

Now for each of the examples find words for how you would express a guess to the person who said them. Use your guesses of what their needs and feelings are for support. Below you will find one example of how you could respond with empathy to the first two sentences:

1."Is it that you really want to be sure that you'll be heard about how this has affected you?"

2. *"Are you scared/concerned about how this will go and want to know whether there is enough support and knowledge before you start?*

3.

4.

5.

6.

7.

Reflecting – What have I learned from these exercises?

Spend a moment reflecting on what you have learned so far about listening, translating and reflecting difficult messages. What have you learnt from part 1? What have you learnt from part 2? Maybe you want to repeat the theory of what you have practiced, to further deepen your knowledge.

Practising "Pulling someone by the ear"

This exercise is suitable for practising in a group of (preferably) three people. You get the chance to use words that feel okay for you, as well as getting feedback on how the person you are "pulling by the ear" experiences this (if you don't have a group to practice with, you can use the "Written exercise: Pulling someone by the ear"). These are the roles you take:

Person A = the person who is sharing how the conflict affects him/her.

Person B = the other person who hasn't shared yet.

The Mediator = the one who "pulls B by the ear". The mediator helps person B to hear what person A is saying by asking B to reflect what needs he or she has heard person A express. If this doesn't work immediately, the mediator tries again in a different way.

If you are a group of just two people, pretend that you have a person A. One of you assumes the role of person B and the other one takes the role of the mediator. If your group has more than three people, you have the advantage of having one or two observers who can give valuable feedback.

To get going and get a taste of what situations this tool can be applied to, use the dialogues from the "Written exercise: Pulling someone by the ear".

Start with A expressing something that the mediator tries to hear the feelings and needs behind (as in the previous exercise).The mediator then asks B to reflect back what A was needing.

It is important to remember that even if one of the parties believes that they are being heard by you, it is essential that they also hear each other. It is about both having a sense of being heard by the other party and about taking in the other party's reality. You might ask:

"Are you willing to reflect back, with your own words, what you understand the other person needs?"
Or

"I hear that A really feels upset and wants to find a way to trust in your cooperation. I wonder if you are willing to reflect that back to her, even if you do not agree or understand it fully?"

Do the first part of the exercise, where the mediator listens for A's needs as simply as possible, so that the mediator can practise "pulling by the ear". When you have tried it a few rounds you can make it more challenging for the mediator.

What can you say if person B:

1. Does not reflect back the needs, but instead repeats the criticism he or she heard?

2. Expresses other needs than what person A actually said?

3. Starts talking about himself and his own needs?

4. Says or does something that you dread encountering. It might be something you have heard before or something that you just fear hearing.

Written exercise -
"Pulling someone by the ear"

If you are working alone and want to practise asking someone what he or she has heard someone else say, you can write out a dialogue. You can either work from the dialogues given below, or write your own examples where the mediator has just reflected back the needs that weren't satisfied for person A, and has asked person B to reflect them back directly to person A in his own words.

Situation 1

The Mediator: (addressing person A)
"I understood that you wanted more companionship than you have had so far. Was this what you meant?"

Person A:
"Yes, exactly"

The Mediator: *(addressing person B)*
"I heard that person A really longs for companionship. Now I would like you to tell her what you have heard she needs, so that she gets a confirmation that her needs have been received, okay?"

Person B (tries, but reflects back the criticism he has heard rather than the needs person A expressed):
"You think I am lazy and that I should be home instead of being out doing things on my own."

The Mediator: Write down what the mediator says to try to help person B to reflect back the feelings and needs person A has expressed.

Situation 2

The Mediator: (addressing person A)
"I understood that you wanted more companionship than you have had so far. Was this what you meant?"

Person A:
"Yes, exactly"

The Mediator: (addressing person B)
"I heard that person A really longs for companionship. Now I would like you to tell her what you have heard she needs, so that she gets confirmation that her needs have been received, okay?"

Person B (tries to reflect back but with other needs than what person A has expressed):
"You are frustrated because you don't have so much meaning in your life."

The Mediator: Write down what the mediator says to try to help person B to reflect back the feelings and needs person A has expressed.

Situation 3

The same as in the earlier exercise. This time you practise "pulling person B by the ear" when he starts to talk about himself and his needs instead of reflecting back the needs person A has expressed. Continue the dialogue until person B has repeated the needs.
Person B says for example;
"Yes, but it feels like a prison at home, I want to feel free!"

Situation 4

Do the same as in the earlier exercises. "Pull person B by the ear" when he does something other than reflect back the needs person A has expressed. Practise what you think would be a challenge. Continue the dialogue until person B has repeated the needs.

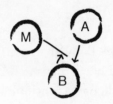

Exercise in interrupting

If in the previous exercise you experienced it a challenge for you to interrupt, it might be beneficial for you to investigate what could make it easier for you. This exercise is best suited to practise with others, preferably in groups of at least three people. In it you will have the opportunity to express yourself out loud, find words that you are comfortable using, and receive feedback on how it feels to the person you interrupt. If you are alone you can practise this technique by writing down the dialogue.

The roles you can use

Person A = the person who at the moment is sharing how the conflict affects him/her.

Person B = the other party who hasn't yet shared his thoughts.

The mediator = interrupts in order to protect the dialogue.

If there are only two people undertaking the exercise, imagine that you have a person A. One of you takes the role of person B and the other the role of the mediator. If there are more than three people in your group, then you have the advantage of having one or two observers who can provide feedback on how this is experienced by others.

Before you start, it's a good idea to prepare a few different ways of interrupting to try out during the role-play. Examples of different situations you could practise are shown below.

Person A talks and the mediator listens. At the same time person B suddenly begins talking. Choose what you want to practise for each new role-play round. You can choose your own examples or use some of the examples below.

It could for example be that person B:

- Is annoyed and angry, perhaps making threats and demands.

- Is arguing and wants to prove that he or she is right.

- Takes the blame, gets embarrassed, and asks for forgiveness.

- Create examples of your own for how the person you want to practice on could react or say.

When person B begins to speak, interrupt and return the focus to person A. Try several different strategies on how to do this. Change roles so that everyone gets the chance to try how it feels. Remember that depending on the intensity of the dialogue, the mediator can interrupt in a rather forceful way using body language to illustrate what is said.

It is important that you as a mediator are clear that the intention of the interruption is to *protect* the dialogue and not to punish or criticize someone. If you are clear about this, the person you interrupt will usually understand that you are doing this to maintain the connection between the parties.
One way of doing this could be to say:
"I can only listen to one person at a time and I would like to finish hearing what person A has to say before I listen to you, is this okay?"

Or
"STOP! I want to finish listening to what person A says before we come to you, okay!?!"
When interrupting, one of the most important things to remember is that the intention is not to silence the person, but rather to protect the flow of information between the parties. This is an essential difference which is often noticed by the person you interrupt through body language such as gestures or a gaze. Try doing this in various ways when you are in the training situation and not in the actual mediation process.

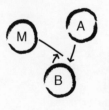

Writing exercise in interrupting

If you're alone and want to practise, you could write out that part of the dialogue. You can work from the example dialogues below or write your own dialogues where person A and person B manage to say something before the mediator interrupts.

Situation 1

Person A:
"You just can't be trusted. People like you should..."

Person B starts talking in a sarcastic tone while person A is still talking):

"And you're so reliable yourself? What abou last year with...?!"

Write down what the mediator can say to interrupt and to bring the focus back to what person A was trying to express:

A Helping Hand
Mediation with Nonviolent Communication

Situation 2

Person A:

"He will never understand how this has been for me anyway. He is such an egoist and only interested in himself and..."

Person B (starts talking while person A is still talking):
"I'm so tired of hearing your analysis of how I am. You sound like a victim and seem to believe that it's only you who..."

Write down what the mediator can say to interrupt respectfully and then bring back the focus to what person A was trying to express:

Situation 3 (your own example)

Person A:

Person B (starts expressing himself/herself while person A is still talking):

Write down what the mediator can say to interrupt respectfully and then bring back the focus to what person A was trying to express:

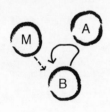

Exercise in interrupting and giving first aid-empathy

When people have pain built up over many years they are so often filled with their own pain that it gets in the way of their hearing another.
Marshall Rosenberg[1]

If person B repeatedly, within a short time, starts talking while person A is speaking, it can be necessary to briefly listen with empathy to person B whom you, as mediator, have interrupted.

This exercise is best suited for group work, preferably with three people. You get to practice words and expressions you feel comfortable using as well as receiving feedback on how they sound for the person who is being interrupted.

The roles to be taken

Person A = the person who at the moment is sharing how the conflict affects him/her.

Person B = the other party who has not shared their thoughts and feelings about the situation yet.

The mediator = who interrupts and offers first aid-empathy.

If there are just two people, imagine that you have a person A, then one of you takes the role as person B and the other the role of the mediator. If there are more than three people in your group, you have the advantage of having one or two observers who can give additional feedback.

Before you start, feel free to prepare a few different ways of interrupting you can try out during the role-play. You can, with the same intention, use the examples from the written exercise on the next double page in order to get ideas about how to get going.

1 Rosenberg, Marshall (2008), Vi kan reda ut det, fredliga sätt att hantera konflikter. Friare Liv Konsult.

Person A expresses him/herself. You're focusing on listening to this when person B suddenly starts to say something. Decide in advance what you want to practise. For example, it could be that person B:

— **Is upset and angry.**

— **Wants to convince you that his/her argument is the right one.**

— **Takes the blame upon himself/herself and asks the other party for forgiveness.**

Write down some of your own examples as to how the person you want to practise on could act or say.

When person B starts to talk; interrupt, offer first aid-empathy and return the focus to person A again. Take the chance to practise many different ways to do this in order to maximize your learning.

Keep in mind that the emotional intensity could be high and the mediator may need to interrupt in a forceful way. As in the previous exercise it is important that you are clear that the purpose of this is to protect the dialogue and not to punish the person or quiet him or her. With this attitude it is also easier to guess what is going on in person B. Make sure to set the exercise at a level of difficulty where everyone has maximum learning opportunities, neither making it too hard nor too easy for each person.

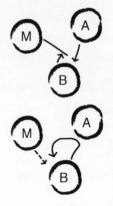

Writing exercise - in interrupting and giving first aid-empathy

If you are practising alone, write down how it could sound when you as a mediator interrupt, and how it could sound when you give first aid-empathy in different dialogues. You could work from the example dialogues below or write your own dialogues where person A and person B manage to say something before the mediator interrupts.

Situation 1

Person A:
"It would have been so different if only you had thought about anyone else but yourself. But you just don't see further than your own nose, it's just you and your..."

Person B: (suddenly starts speaking while person A is still talking and objects A):
"I don't do anything else than think about you, but you are never satisfied, so it doesn't matter whatever I say and ..."

Write down what the mediator could say (interrupting both person A and B and bringing back the focus/attention to what person A was trying to express).
One way of doing this could be:
"I guess you are feeling really irritated right now and want to be sure to be heard as well.? [Short break] I want to listen to A so that I can understand what needs she is trying to express, and I would like to listen to you after that. Okay?"

Situation 2

Person A:
"You have to understand you can't go on like this! It's completely..." "

Person B (angry and upset suddenly starts speaking while person A is still talking):
"I'm so tired of hearing your idiotic advice, you can JUST FORGET that I..."

Write down what the mediator could say (interrupting and bringing back the focus to what person A was trying to express).

Situation 3 (your own example)

Choose a reply to person A and person B:
Person B suddenly starts speaking while person A still is talking.

Write down what the mediator could say (interrupting and bringing back the focus to what person A was trying to express).

Reflecting

What have I learned? Spend a moment reflecting on what you have learned from this. You may want to reread the text in chapter 6 on interrupting in order to further anchor your knowledge. Consider what you find the most difficult and what you want to practise more. What could you do to learn more, what ways of practising could you create?

(If you notice that you still find interrupting a challenge you may benefit from doing the following in depth exercises on interrupting.)

In depth exercise in interrupting

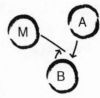

This is a self-reflective exercise to investigate what prevents you from interrupting when it would be constructive for the mediation to do so. Take time to write down the answers to the questions and you will eventually have an idea about which of your needs could be active in these situations. You don't have to choose situations from a mediation, the most important thing is that you connect with what happens in you when you interrupt others or when someone interrupts you. This applies to all of the questions except the last one which is about how an interruption can affect the mediation dialogue.

1a. Imagine a situation where you want to interrupt and find it a challenge to do so. How is it for you to interrupt? How do you feel when you think of interrupting?

b. Which of your needs do you believe might not be met by doing so?

c. Which of your needs could be met by it?

d. Try to put yourself in the other person's situation. How do you think that person would feel if you interrupted them? And what needs of that person do you think would be met and not met if you interrupted?

e. Is there anything about your way of interrupting that you could change? Something that you think would have made a difference in the previous situation? Is there anything you could do differently that would be more satisfying for both parties?

2a. Think back to a situation when someone else started to talk while you were talking, a time when you did not appreciate it. How did you feel?

b. Which of your needs weren't met?

c. Which of your needs were met?

d. If you try to put yourself in the other person's situation, which of that person's needs do you think was or was not met by you interrupting?

3. Imagine a mediation situation where you interrupt someone because you want to make sure the other party gets heard before you shift focus. The person reacts in a way that is challenging for you. What could help you keep or repair the connection with someone who reacts in this way?

4. In order to identify more judgements that you may be unaware of that are affecting your ability to interrupt when it would be constructive, you could answer the following questions:

a. Finish the following sentences with whatever answer comes to mind:

- A person who interrupts is...

- If I interrupt, I am as.... (judgement) as...(name).

- To interrupt is...

- People who interrupt should...

- If she interrupts me one more time then...

- If you interrupt you have to...

b. What feelings and needs are behind each of these finished sentences?

5. What have you learned from this exercise? What can you do to become more effective in interrupting?

Practising Self-Empathy during mediation

Part 1: When you judge yourself in ways that makes it hard for you to mediate

Certain thoughts can be a challenge to handle during a meditation session. Think about things such as inner criticism, demands, expectations and interpretations that you will want to quickly let go of in order to refocus on the two parties and the mediation again.

Examples of self-judgments could be:

1. I'll never manage this!

2. This will never work, I should be more... (Analysis of own ability).

3. This is going to be a fiasco! I have to try to find a smart solution before it is too late.

Write down your own judgments, interpretations, comparisons etc.

4. I am _____ (labels, judgments, comparisons, analyses).

5. I must _____ (expectations and demands).

6. If I don't _____ (threats)!

7. Other _____

Translate each of the above finished sentences into feelings and needs:

1. *I'll never manage this!*
*What feelings are behind this?*_____

*What needs?*_____

Feeling: Nervousness, concern?

Need: Trust, to contribute?

2. *This will never work, I should be more... (Analysis of own ability).*

*What feelings are behind this?*_____

*What needs?*_____

3. *This is going to be a fiasco! I have to try to find a smart solution before it is too late.*

*Feeling?*_____

*Need?*_____

4. *I am* _____ *(labels, judgments, comparisons, analyses)*

*Feeling?*_____

*Need?*_____

5. *I must* _____ *(expectations and demands)*

*Feeling?*_____

*Need?*_____

6. *If I don't* _____ *(threats)!*

Feeling?

Need?

7. *Other* _____

Feeling?

Need?

Then frame how you could express guesses using those feelings and needs. Take some time for each of your guesses to sink in. It is connection you want, which doesn't necessarily mean the guesses are completely right. Creating connection with yourself during a mediation situation can enable you to continue even when it is a challenge to do it:

Example 1: *I'll never manage this!*

My own self-empathy guess:
"When I connect with myself, I notice that I feel nervous and concerned. Maybe it is because I want to trust that what I do really is a contribution?

Part 2: When you judge the parties in ways that makes it hard for you to mediate

Another situation where it is invaluable that you hear yourself with empathy is when you have strong judgements about one or both of the parties. If you can hear your own opinions with empathy, it usually becomes easier to accept them and not be disrupted by them. Learning to quickly translate the inner criticism into unmet needs takes less energy. You can more easily focus on what you believe leads to a satisfying mediation.

Examples of judgements, interpretations etc about the involved parties:

1. "No wonder they don't get together/agree the way they behave."

2. "Why don't they just give up? Now they have to stop! Can't they hear how they sound?!"

3. "These people are hopeless."

4. "She's going to get mad at me if I interrupt again."

Write down your own judgements, interpretations, comparisons etc.

5. They are/he is/she is _____ (labels, judgements, analyses)

6. They/he/she should _____ (expectations and demands)

7. If they don't _____ *then* _____(threat)!

8. Other_____

Translate each of the sentences above into feelings and needs:

Example:

1. "No wonder they are not able to get things to work. They should both shape up"

What are the feelings behind what is said _____?

What is the need behind what is said _____?

Feeling: Do I feel annoyed and powerless?

Need: Maybe I have a need for hope that people can find ways to connect?

Take a deep breath, and let each of your guesses sink in. Even if it's not entirely correct, the decision to listen to yourself with empathy can be beneficial for your ability to be present. To connect with what is important for you can make it easier to let go of strong judgments about the parties, which will help you to continue the mediation dialogue.

2. *"They have to stop this! Can't they hear that they sound like idiots?!"*

Feeling?

Need?

3. "These people are hopeless."

Feeling?

Need?

4. *"She's going to get mad at me if I interrupt again."*
Feeling?
Need?

5. *They are/he is/she is* _____ (labels, judgements, analyses)
Feeling?
Need?

6. They/he/she should _____ (expectations and demands)
Feeling?
Need

7. *If they don't* _____ *then* _____(threat)!
Feeling?
Need

A Helping Hand
Mediation with Nonviolent Communication

8. Other_____
Feeling?
Need?

Then formulate how you could express guesses to yourself with the help of the feelings and needs you found above. Give yourself some time to allow your guesses to fully sink in and help you deepen your self-connection. If you notice that you are making recurring judgements in mediation situations, it could be invaluable to identify in what kind of situation this happens so that you can catch those judgements more quickly. That is, what the parties or yourself say or do just at the moment when these thoughts are stimulated.

Reflecting -What did I learn from the exercises I just did?

Spend a moment reflecting about what you have learned on self-empathy.
What did you learn from Part 1? From Part 2? Maybe you want to repeat the theory surrounding what you have practised in order to further anchor your knowledge.

Exercise in tracking needs

During a mediation, the pace of the dialogue can become rather fast, with interruptions from the different parties, strong emotional expressions, and also new tracks that turn up before the earlier ones have been taken care of. Because of this, it is important to find ways to track whose needs are "on the table" and to be able to take care of them when it is possible.

To practise this ability to track [needs] you can use any group situation. It could be about a group you belong to, a conversation at work or in the family, or you could even practice while watching a situation in a TV-series or movie. During a mediation several things are often happening at the same time; you need to be attentive as a mediator. So take as many opportunities as possible to practise – this skill will be much needed and utilized when you act as a third party.

Choose a situation to practice with. Before starting the exercise you might want to decide how long you wish to spend on it. Feel free to have pens and paper available and write down your answers to make them even clearer.

Ask yourself:

1a. Whose needs are on the table right now? What needs?

b. Whose needs are on the table right now? What needs?

c. Whose needs are on the table right now? What needs?

2a. What needs have been/ have not been taken care of? What have you seen that makes you think that?

b. What needs have been/ have not been taken care of? What have you seen that makes you think that?

c. What needs have been/ have not been taken care of? What have you seen that makes you think that?

A Helping Hand
Mediation with Nonviolent Communication

Reflection about tracking

When you finish, take some time to reflect over and write down what you have learned by observing the flow when following how needs are handled. For example, think about what led you to feel the way you did during the process. Perhaps you became confused, annoyed, happy, bored or calm. It can be important to connect with those of your needs that these feelings show you, as they may affect you during a future mediation.

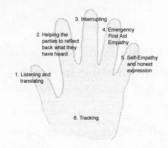

Exercise informal mediation - in slow motion

You have now had the opportunity to practise using several different tools during mediation. Maybe you haven't as yet gotten a clear picture of how mediation can be carried out, or don't yet have the courage to try mediating in a real situation. The following exercise could be the next step. You can do it either on your own or in a group. It may not reflect a complete mediation session if that could take more time than you or the group want to devote to the exercise. If you use this as a group exercise you will have the opportunity to listen at a slow pace to what is being said by any of the parties and to practice handling whatever comes up. You also will have the possibility to explore how the course of events can change depending on how people are being received.

If you work in a group you may let one person play the role of person A, one person play the role of person B and the rest of the group act as mediator. Getting really into these roles can make it easier to imagine what the different parts might express.

Choose a situation in which the mediator isn't invited to mediate, but chooses to do so because he or she thinks mediation can help. The mediation could be a conflict in your family, at your work, between people who have different viewpoints regarding cooperation, raising children, religion, politics or environmental issues. The situation can be made up or based on something that has actually happened. Agree on who plays the two parties. If there are several people doing the exercise together it could be beneficial to have a flip-chart or a large poster-size paper where you can write down the dialogue. You can use the schedule "Five Steps in Mediation" and "Reminders for the mediator" in chapter 8 for support during the exercise.

A Helping Hand
Mediation with Nonviolent Communication

a. Write down what person A says.

b. Write down what the mediator could answer.

c. Write down what happens after this; it could be person A or B who says something.

d. Write down how the mediator responds to whatever has been said.

Continue the dialogue as long as it seems meaningful. If you want to increase the level of difficulty you could let person B start talking at the same time as person A. In this way you can get practise interrupting and offering first aid empathy.

Chapter 8

Formal mediation

To mediate after being invited to do so

What I mean by formal mediation is when you are invited as a third party to mediate in a conflict. It can be easier to mediate when you have been formally invited to do so, since both parties are more prepared and more willing to receive support. Also, you can create a clear structure for the talk right from the start, which can facilitate the parties listening to and understanding each other. At a formal mediation, it is almost always possible to begin by briefly explaining how the role of mediator works.

One challenge in being a third party during a formal mediation is that many wait a long time before asking for support in a conflict. As a consequence, there can be very strong emotions involved. When the parties have felt unhappy during a longer period of time, the conflict may have escalated significantly. Held-back emotions can explode like a volcano during a mediation. If a situation has become very infected or if the participants have a lot of prestige invested in the outcome, it can be a great challenge to open up and get support from a mediator in communicating.

Below are some examples of what a mediator can say at the beginning of a formal mediation. Remember though that it may be difficult for an upset person to take in information, so keep the introduction as brief as possible. It is up to you to decide what is important to include in the introduction.

The way you present yourself "sets the tone" for the mediation. You might want to say something personal about yourself, why you do mediation or how you feel right now, since this often contributes to security.

Sometimes it is also useful to say a few things about the background leading up to the mediation. For example, you can say something about how you were contacted, with which people you have spoken to and what information you have received. Perhaps you want to give the parties a chance to correct or add to the information you may have already received. Describing the background to the mediation can serve as an opportunity to verify that the facts are correct while ensuring that everyone involved knows who initiated the mediation.

Facing a workplace conflict, it is not unusual for parties to worry that the mediator has a hidden agreement with a stakeholder in the conflict, such as a senior executive. There might also be concerns that the mediator has been given a distorted view of the situation, having spoken to only some of the people involved.

Giving the parties written information about how mediation can work often contributes to security and clarity. This can increase their understanding of your role in managing the conflict. If the parties receive written information prior to the mediation, they can read through in peace and quiet. They will have an easier time getting used to the idea of mediation, as well as being able to prepare questions or requests. There is an example of such information in the box on the next page.

A Helping Hand
Mediation with Nonviolent Communication

What happens during a mediation

1. The role of the mediator is to help parties in a conflict to find ways to deal with what is being experienced as a challenge. Since the mediator's main function is to help you create connection, the mediator may sometimes rephrase something that is said. The aim is to make it easier for others to hear it, without of course, distorting the message.

2. The mediator will ask you to express which needs you want to have met in your relationship, what you long for and what you would like to be different after the mediation.

3. The mediator will not focus directly on solutions. Instead, the mediator will first ask you to express your needs and then listen to the other party's needs. When you are connected with each other's needs, finding solutions that suit everyone will be much easier.

4. The mediator will ask you to reflect back the needs that the other party is expressing, making sure that the message has been received and that the connection has been strengthened.

5. The mediator can obviously only listen to one party at a time. However, the mediator does not intend to take anyone's side. When one party has been heard, the mediator will turn to the other party so that everyone can be heard.

6. The mediator can help you to rephrase unclear or vague requests into agreements that are more workable.

7. The mediator may interrupt if he or she thinks that something that is being said may threaten your connection.

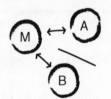

Meeting with the parties before the mediation

Whenever possible, it is useful to meet with the parties individually before the actual mediation talk. Preparatory meetings give the parties an opportunity to reflect on what has happened, why it happened and to gain some distance from the situation. It may make it easier for you as a mediator to decide how you want to start, and if there is anything that needs some extra attention.

It can also be helpful to have talked through whether or not you want to agree upon how you want the mediation to be run. Such agreements can create security and support you in leading the mediation. This can be especially important during a mediation between people who have physically hurt or threatened each other. You can find additional material about this in the paragraph with the title "A sense of free choice - a prerequisite for a successful mediation" later in this chapter.

If you have been contacted by one party you can, during a preparatory meeting with the other party, ask if he or she has experienced freedom of choice regarding participation. Perhaps you won't get a direct answer, but their answers to other questions can reveal if they feel forced to participate. For example, feeling forced to participate can be revealed when you talk about how it feels to have been asked to take part in the mediation, or how it felt to be contacted by you.

It can be valuable to touch on why you were the one asked to mediate and what the mediation may cost. If there is work of a confidential nature (typical in some professions), it may be important to talk about how you want to approach this during the course of the mediation. You may also want to give them information about how you act as a mediator and the way a mediation process works. This can be done in writing or you can inform them verbally and give them a chance to ask questions. Remember that it is often just as important to address their concerns with empathy, as it is to give them more information.

If you notice that someone is having second thoughts about participating, take some time to figure out what is going on. There may be fear and uncertainty about what the mediation might lead to, pain about the conflict having gone this far, or sometimes embarrassment and shame

A Helping Hand
Mediation with Nonviolent Communication

about having to reach out for support.

Some things to talk about during a preparatory meeting:

– What they want to get out of the mediation. What needs they want to find new strategies for.

– Why you will sometimes ask one of them to wait to speak until the other party has been heard.

– Why you will ask them to restate the needs that they have heard the other party say that they want to have met in their connection.

– If they have any feelings of doubt over participating.

I was asked to mediate in a workgroup in town. The group consisted of middle level managers who for a long time had found it very challenging to find ways to cooperate both with each other and with other workgroups they were in charge of. The conflict had escalated to the point where some no longer talked to each other.

During the first preparatory meeting with some of them and their immediate supervisor, it became clear that two of the middle level managers had expressed that they did not want to be a part of any mediation. This in turn had led to a lot of discouragement among others in the group who said things like:

"If they don't participate the whole idea will fall apart, and there is no point in me spending time on this either."

We realized that the mediation preparations had gone too fast, and that the process was not entirely established. Therefore, we decided that I would have more individual talks with some of the managers before we decided whether or not to have a mediation talk with the entire team.

I first met with those who had said that they did not want to participate. During one meeting, it came to my attention that the person I was meeting with viewed the person who had proposed the mediation as his biggest "rival". He thought that she had made the proposal as a way of getting at him, to discredit him. When he realized that I was not there on behalf of that person, but rather to listen to all sides, he said yes to participation. Also, when he realized that he really was free to choose to walk away if he didn't want to stay, it became much easier for him to say yes to the mediation.

In my conversation with the other person, I learned that she had not understood that it was important to others if she did or did not participate. She was a relatively new employee and believed she had nothing to contribute. For her, it was easy to choose to participate when I told her how the others had reacted when they heard that she was not planning on participating.

Without these conversations, we might have given up, running the risk of increasing the conflict. We might have tried to carry out the mediation with those who had chosen to stay. If we had chosen the latter option we would have made some progress, but would still have risked ending up focusing on expressing disappointment that not everyone wanted to participate, rather than focusing on managing the actual conflict.

The mediator's preparations

You can prepare yourself for a formal mediation in several ways. A first step is to obtain information about the background to the conflict. Another step is becoming clear about your own internal process. It is easy to spend all your time and energy preparing yourself for dealing with the content or format of the mediation. However, be sure to also set aside time to prepare yourself for your own emotional process, in order to contribute to an optimal result.

Background information

Approaching some mediation talks, you can benefit from some background information about the conflict. When I mediate in a work group, the supervisor or some other employer sometimes wants to give his or her view of the people involved before I meet them. Previously, I would sometimes listen to this, but I now nearly always decline. I have learned that the fewer static images I have of the people involved, the more effective I am as mediator.

There may be differences that are valuable to pay attention to and understand when you do mediation talks with people from different cultures. However, note that even within a culture there are great individual differences. Every idea of how a person from a certain culture should act, think or communicate, can prevent you from really seeing this person. The more you can focus on getting in touch with the needs we all have, regardless of culture, religion, occupation, age or gender, the more likely you can contribute towards cooperation. In the book *"Getting to Yes"*, a situation is described where things got very bad:

> *For example, in Persian, the word "compromise" apparently lacks the positive meaning it has in English of "a midway solution both sides can live with," but has only a negative meaning as in "her virtue was compromised" or "our integrity was compromised." Similarly, the word "mediator" in Persian suggests "meddler," someone who is barging in uninvited. In early 1980 U.N. Secretary General Waldheim flew to Iran to deal with a hostage situation. His efforts were seriously set back when Iranian national radio and television broadcast in Persian a remark he reportedly made on his arrival in Tehran: "I have come as a mediator" to work out a "compromise." Within an hour of the broadcast, his car was being stoned by angry Iranians.[1]*

Preparation - Inner clarity

You can prepare yourself for a formal mediation in several ways. A first step is to obtain information about the background to the conflict. Another step is becoming clear about your own internal process. It is easy to spend all your time and energy preparing yourself for dealing with the content or format of the mediation. However, be sure to also set aside time to prepare yourself for your own emotional process, in order to contribute towards an optimal result. The next page contains a series of questions designed to help you prepare to mediate.

Determining what these ideas represent to you is one of the most important preparations you can make. When you are connected with the needs behind these ideas, they provide valuable information that can strengthen your presence during the mediation talk. In addition to answering the questions on the next page, you can use other parts of the book as preparation.

---

1 Fisher & Ury(1987), *Getting to Yes.* Arrow Books Limited.

- Read the paragraph on self-empathy in Chapter 6 on page 106.

- Use the exercise "Self-empathy during mediation" in Chapter 7 on page 146.

- Read the paragraph "Prepare yourself to mediate" in Chapter 8 on page 165.

- Do the exercise "Be clear about your purpose in mediating" in Chapter 7 on page 119.

Prepare yourself to mediate

If you are under stress, it is useful to set aside some time to slow down before the mediation. The following questions can help you get better connected with yourself, which helps you become more aware of how you can contribute to the mediation process.

Inner preparation

1. What labels do I have of the participants?
2. What labels do I have of myself?
3. Am I unconsciously demanding anything from any of the participants?
4. Am I unconsciously demanding anything from myself?
5. Am I doubtful whether everyone experiences that they are voluntarily participating?
6. Am I experiencing that I am voluntarily acting as a third party?
7. What is my purpose in mediating?
8. Am I locked into a certain solution to the conflict or am I open to the solution possibly being very different than anything I had in mind?

Outer preparation

1. Do I need more information about the people that are participating in the mediation?
2. Do I need more information about the background to the conflict?
3. Do I need more information about why I was invited to mediate?
4. Do the parties have enough information about how mediation works? Have we had as many preliminary meetings as needed?

The sense of free choice -a prerequisite for a successful mediation

If it is clear from the start of a mediation that everyone is participating voluntarily, you have created a good situation for success. One of the reasons why it is difficult to establish connection with or between the parties during a mediation is an experience of demand by the parties. Difficulties can also stem from the mediator believing that mediation is the only way to handle the conflict.

Depending upon who invited you to mediate and on whose behalf you are mediating will also affect whether the mediation is perceived as a free choice or not. If, for example, an employer has invited you to mediate but has not confirmed the decision within the work group, employees can easily think that they have no chance to say no. They might join the mediation because they are worried about the consequences, not because they really care if the connection is improved or if a solution to the conflict is found.

It is helpful if both you and the parties are open to the idea that there are other ways of dealing with conflicts than carrying out mediation talks. Ensuring that there are other options often contributes to a greater experience of free choice. When people participate because they think it is their duty, or because they want to avoid guilt or shame, the mediation can end up dealing with their reluctance. There is also a risk that all cards won't be put on the table, because it is usually not easy to be open and honest when you experience duty or demand.

Although voluntary participation is important, it is also important to give information about how a person's decision not to take part in a mediation can affect others. Many people do not understand that their presence can be a gift to others, and that a decision not to participate can have a greater impact than they realize. There is a major difference between people participating in a mediation because they want to experience that they are contributing to others, and people participating because they think it is their duty or obligation to do so.

If you for some reason get stuck on the idea that mediation is the best and only way to deal with conflicts, it is useful to examine why you think this. Is there a strong desire to make a difference or a concern about what will happen if the parties do not connect with each other?

A Helping Hand
Mediation with Nonviolent Communication

If someone hears demands and rebels

As a mediator, it is useful to be extra aware of people hearing what others are saying as demands, because freedom and choice are such important needs for us humans. Since these needs are so central, agreements that contain demands are usually not followed in the long run.

As long as people hear demands, they can only act in two ways: they can rebel and go against the demand they hear, or they can give in and submit to the demand. Both ways can make it more difficult for the parties to reach a resolution to the conflict, since the mediation becomes a game of "either-or".

Someone has probably heard a demand if they are thinking or saying:
"I'll never agree to that!"

Or:
"That is absurd, how can you demand such a thing!"

Or more vaguely:
"That's not normal!"

Two of the basic assumptions that NVC is based on (and described in more detail in Chapter 5) can be very useful here:
1. Everything humans do, they do with the intention to try to meet their needs.

2. People want to contribute to others if they feel that they are doing so voluntarily.

As a mediator, you can rely on these principles in order to hear the needs expressed in the sentences above, for example by guessing:
"Are you worried because you have a need to choose for yourself how you want to do things?"

Or:
"You want to make sure that what you want in this situation is clear to everyone involved?"

Since we can always choose how we hear something, you can help the party who hears demands to focus instead on both what they themselves want and on the needs of the person who "is making the demand". Avoid discussing or arguing about whether it was a demand or not, because this rarely leads to connection.

If someone hears demands and "gives in"

If you as a mediator believe that either party thinks that they are being forced to agree on something, both care and clarification from the mediator may be required in order to move forward. Depending on what the situation calls for, you might want to ask:

"I feel a bit worried when I hear you say yes to the proposal, because I have previously heard you really stress your dissatisfaction with it. I want to make sure that you have the support you need in order to avoid going along with something you don't want. So I am wondering if you'd like to say something about why you are now saying yes to the proposal?"

Hopefully, the question may help the person to be open about what is going on. However, in some situations, where there are spoken or unspoken threats, the person may have a need for more security. One way of helping the person dare to express him- or herself more openly is by listening to the parties one at a time. To put their fears into words and to have these fears heard can make a big difference in such a situation.

The neutral mediator

In mediation literature and mediation trainings, the importance of being neutral as a mediator is often emphasized. On the one hand, I am in agreement about the value of being able to remain neutral, of not taking sides as a mediator. On the other hand, I am not sure if we humans can ever be completely neutral.

When I hear mediators say that they will be completely neutral during a mediation, I am often skeptical and wonder what they mean. I gain more confidence that the mediator will be attentive of himself or herself in a way that can support the mediation, if the mediator says that he or she has the intention to really listen to both sides and not to take sides. It also worries me if the mediator thinks it is wrong or bad to take sides. With this attitude, taking sides easily becomes taboo, resulting in a greater risk that the mediator can deny some things that are going on.

There are several things you can do when you find that you are stuck in thoughts about "this party is actually right". One way of evaluating whether or not you think this will affect your ability to listen and understand both sides, is to connect with the needs that lie behind your thoughts about who is right.

When it is clear which needs you have that have not been met, you can usually be able to continue the mediation. Learn more about this in Chapter 7, in the paragraph about pitfalls, and in the exercises on self-empathy.

Sometimes the mediation process may benefit when you express the needs that have influenced you to take sides. At other times, a better option would be to take a break so that you can be heard with empathy by someone, and then evaluate how to proceed. You can also cancel the mediation if you think that what is going on inside of you will stand in the way of your ability to hear both sides.

Two mediators or one?

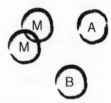

Sometimes it is useful to have two mediators instead of one. Two people notice different things which can provide more ways of looking at how the conflict can be dealt with. Two mediators also makes it easier to break up a mediation and listen to the two separate parties in situations where this is more effective. If one mediator starts taking sides, the other mediator will hopefully see this, and can ensure that both parties' needs are taken into consideration. In situations where threats or violence has occurred, two mediators often create more security.

Also, two mediators can contribute to an experience of greater freedom for the mediators, since one of them may be able to take a break, while the other can continue the mediation.

There are, of course, pitfalls in having two mediators. Once when I was working with another mediator in a work group, three of the people in the work group expressed that it felt unsafe having two mediators. They felt that we had a strong impact on the situation, making it difficult for them to dare to express themselves. We solved this by having only one of us talking and the other sitting as an observer with a clear agreement only to act when requested to.

The place for the mediation

At a formal mediation, the mediator may sometimes have a chance to influence where the mediation will take place. Be attentive when choosing the location, especially if you think you might be perceived as taking sides by suggesting a place where one party feels more at home than the other. Choosing a suitable location can be an important first step in creating a "neutral" starting point for a mediation.

Also consider seating positions. It helps if the parties can see each other when talking. Seat them at the same height, since height difference often is perceived as a power marker.

The start of the mediation

The mediator might begin the mediation talk by saying:
"Thank you for coming. My hope is to help create connection between you so that you can reach a solution together. I have met with each of you for 30 minutes at some time during the past week. I have been asked to mediate by your boss."

He or she can then continue by saying:
"I'll begin by asking you to express what you need in relation to the other party. I will not focus on a solution or on taking sides. I will primarily be focusing on your connection. I want to listen to you one at a time, so that everyone can be heard. If I hear you express something I think will stand in the way of your connection, I will help you to find other ways of expressing the same thing. My hope is that this will make it easier for you to truly hear each other - since being heard and understood is an important part of mediation. I'll interrupt you if I get worried that something being said will make it more difficult to connect. Do you have any questions or can we agree to start like this?"

A Helping Hand
Mediation with Nonviolent Communication

If you have made these points clear and the participants have agreed to you rephrasing difficult messages, they tend to have an easier time dealing with it. You might want to briefly share your understanding of what has happened. Remember that even if it is sometimes useful to clarify the background, it is often a challenge for the parties to agree on the description of the background. It is usually more efficient to focus directly on listening to their feelings and needs.

Who starts?

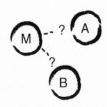

"I would like to hear what needs you would like to have met in this situation. Who wants to start by expressing what they would like?"

Sometimes you want to exert more influence over who starts talking than you can get with this open-ended question. For example, you can turn directly to the person you are guessing is experiencing most pain about the situation. Or you might want to start with the person you think is least motivated to participate.

If you already think that one party is having trouble hearing the other, you can turn directly to that party and ask:

"I wonder if you want to be the one who starts by telling us which of your needs are not being met in this situation?"

When you use the latter option, make sure to notice whether the other person feels that you are "taking sides" or is worried that he or she won't get as much space as the first person. You can also start from any of the following suggestions if you want to influence who starts:

1. Start with the party you feel will have the most difficulties in hearing the other person.

2. Start with the person you lack connection with, in order to get better connected.

3. Start with the person you think is most ready to begin. This is particularly useful in situations which are very loaded, where no one seems to want to open up. Once a person has begun talking it may help the other to continue.

4. Start with the party you think will put a lot of energy into defending what he or she has done. If you don't do this there is a risk that the person will be preoccupied with preparing what he or she wants to say, rather than just listening.

Note that in mediation concerning restorative justice or mediation in crime, there are set structures about who starts sharing.

Time frames

Especially during formal mediation, there are often time frames to consider. Be sure that there is time left at the end to determine the next step together, for example to arrange a follow-up meeting.

If time runs out during a point in the mediation where many things are still in progress, you can, of course, ask if the parties are able to continue.

If you want to meet on more occasions, perhaps you can make some common agreements about various actions the parties might do until the next meeting.

Things to agree on can, for example, include avoiding meeting each other (or not), talking about the conflict with each other (or not), or whether to perform some particular action as a first step in repairing what has happened (or not). In order to create safety, you might want to be a bit more active here by suggesting ways to deal with the situation.

Solutions and agreements

When you feel that a stable connection between the parties has been established, you can change focus towards supporting them in finding a solution.

One way of determining if it is time to change focus is to sense if you are experiencing some sort of emotional shift within yourself. You can find out if this it true for the parties as well, by asking a question such as:

"Now that you have heard how this situation has impacted on both of you, can anyone imagine a way to handle this that could satisfy everyone's needs?"

Remember to drop any ideas about some kind of ultimate goal or "best solution". Conflicts can give rise to completely different agreements than thought of at the beginning of the conversation.

If you think that it is your job as a mediator to resolve the conflict, mediation can feel like quite a heavy load to carry. You may or may not find a solution.

The parties can usually find a solution for themselves. They often have a much better overall picture than you will ever have and therefore are in a better position to make arrangements that really work. Also, people are more often likely to keep agreements if they themselves are responsible for coming up with them.

As a mediator, you can still be very useful when the parties are formulating clear requests of the other party, or when they are formulating common solutions. This often involves helping the parties to find what they want, rather than what they don't want. You can also be a great source of support if you help the parties translate vague desires into clear requests.

Clear requests can prevent conflicts

If you are concerned about an agreement being so vague and ambiguous that it might lead to future or recurring problems, you can help by reformulating it. It is far more likely that the parties will stick to an agreement that is practical and possible to put into action, than if the agreement is based on what one should not do. Here is an example of such an agreement I once heard in a situation where I mediated between a parent and a teenager. The parent said:

"You can't take money from my wallet without asking!"

In order to make the above statement more clear and practical, and therefore more likely to be followed, it can be formulated into something like this:

"Next time you want money for something I want you to tell me so we can deal with it together. How do you feel thinking about doing that?"

This request makes it clearer what the person wants. The request is expressed in a way that also takes the other person's needs into account. Now it is much more likely that the other person will want to do what I ask him or her to do. This way we can ensure that the agreement is based on something both parties are willing to accept.

If we are not sure whether the parties feel completely free to express themselves, or don't have confidence that they will be heard if they answer no, we can also end by saying:

"...Is there anything you need right now in order to say yes to this?"

With this additional question we get a chance to remove obstacles or to improve the agreement. In this way, we are increasing the likelihood that it will be followed. There are variations to this question that may help us gain access to even more information:

"...Is there anything you can think of that could make it difficult for you to ask me for money next time?"

Or:

"...Is there anything I can do to make it easier for you to ask me for money next time you need something?"

When attention is put on "not taking money from my wallet," there are many other ways in which the teenager in this story can act. Some of these may be even less attractive than what we wish the teenager to refrain from doing. For instance, money may be taken from someone else's wallet, or shoplifting something from a store could take place. A specific request, on the other hand, shows more clearly what action the party making a request wants to see happen and an agreement may also be easier to later follow for the person receiving the request.

I have heard people comment on similar situations like the one above by saying for example:

"What is all this pampering about? Just draw the line and show what is wrong!"

However, I maintain that giving a clear and specific request rather than "drawing the line and showing what is wrong" will produce the desired outcome much more effectively. In this particular case, before mediation both the teenager's parents and other adults in positions of authority had tried to force the teenager to stop taking money by proclaiming that taking money without permission was not permitted and threatening punishment unless the behavior was changed. Although the teenager on several occasions agreed to not take money without asking, this behavior continued. Furthermore, since he knew that he ran the risk of being punished for his behavior, he began to avoid telling the truth when confronted, in order to avoid punishment.

People agree on things because they see how the agreement has a potential of meeting their needs. It seems that if people agree on things for other reasons, there is a high risk that the agreement won't be kept. The most successful agreements are the ones that from the start have the intention of meeting everyone's needs and are co-created by the parties.

Focus on the core of the conflict

If you have switched to finding a solution to the conflict and you notice that the parties are losing their connection again, it may help to briefly summarize what seems to be most significant for both of them.

"A, one thing I heard that you really long for is to feel more trust, have I understood that this is what you would like? And B, based on how I have understood you, it is important for you to experience freedom and an opportunity to decide things for yourself."

Or:

"To my understanding, this was the core of the situation when we started the conversation and I want to know if you have an idea of how these needs can be met in a more efficient way than before?"

You may also find that being open about your purpose can lead to deeper connection:

"I am reminding you about this because I get a bit worried that we will lose touch with what is at the heart of the conflict. I believe it will be easier to cooperate around a solution if we remember what is important for both of you."

You can of course continue in many different ways, for example:

"Now you have heard what is important for the other person. Are either of you getting any ideas about how this could be resolved in a way that could work for both of you?"

Or:

"Now that everyone's interests have been expressed, I wonder if anyone has any suggestions on how we can deal with this in a way that you think could satisfy everyone's interests?"

Supporting the parties to fully connect with the core of what is important for both sides can help them to respect the connections they have established. It can also help them to be more open towards new strategies or ways of relating to each other.

After having created deeper connection, the original problem is sometimes not very alive for one or both parties. The connection and mutual care they now experience, and which they have longed for all along, have become the most important concern. To take in that you mean something to someone else can completely change a conflict situation. Even if you guess that this is the case, you can still remind the parties of the original problem:

"Is there anything concerning what you came here with that you still want to find a solution to?"

This is an important question, because the parties can easily lose themselves in the warm feelings that come with having recreated the connection with someone who means a lot to them. If you hear that the parties are hesitant about continuing the mediation, you can also ask:

"I get worried when I hear that you are happy even when you haven't reached a new way to handle this situation. My worry comes from knowing that it can feel so good to finally be connected that we forget the problem until the day it happens again. Therefore I wonder if you, with my help, are willing to take 10 minutes to see if we can reach some agreements regarding how you will handle this if it comes back?"

Of course, it's not enough just to help each side see what the other side needs. We must end with action that meets everybody's needs.
Marshall Rosenberg[1]

After the mediation

Follow-up meetings reinforce the sense that dealing with a conflict does not affect only the parties themselves. At this point, mediation also becomes part of a larger social context. It becomes clear how we are interconnected and how our actions affect others.

An important feature of mediation is to create lasting change. In order to achieve this you need to make agreements that have the potential of meeting the needs of all parties. In this context, follow-up meetings are a valuable aid to track and secure what has happened since the mediation conversation. You can do this individually with one party at a time or with everyone involved simultaneously. As a mediator, you can focus on two things:

1. Ask if the parties' needs have been more satisfied after the mediation. If not, how come? Have new things surfaced where the support of a third-party is needed?

2. Have the agreements made during the mediation been held? If not, how come? Is there any part of the agreement which is vague, unclear, or not possible to act upon? Is there anything the mediator can help to clarify?

---

1 Rosenberg, Marshall (2008), *We Can Work it Out.* Puddle Dancer Press.

Reminders to the mediator

1. Your purpose as a mediator is to support the connection between all parties.

2. Sometimes you will not find solutions that work for everyone; but seeing each other's humanity can deepen the trust between the parties.

3. Instead of getting caught in a game of "Whose fault is it?", emphasize the humanity of both parties.

4. Feelings can be sensitive to express, especially at the beginning of a mediation. As a mediator you can choose to focus on needs instead, and leave out words describing feelings.

5. It can be very challenging for the parties to hear each other. Rephrase what you hear in order to help them.

6. Avoid focusing on "fairness" or "justice"; focus on needs instead.

7. "No" is always a "yes" to something else.

8. Focus on long-term goals rather than on immediate action.

9. Connecting with your own feelings and needs helps you to understand your own reactions and to be more neutral and open.

10. Mediation can be much more chaotic in reality than any model can ever describe.

A Helping Hand
Mediation with Nonviolent Communication

Mediation in five steps

Step	Process	What does the mediator do?
1.	Person A expresses any needs that are not met in the conflict and the emotions it raises.	Can decide who will talk first. Listens and reflects the observations, feelings, needs and requests person A expresses.
2.	Person B reflects the needs Person A expressed, with or without the help of the mediator.	Helps person B reflect back Person A's unmet needs with the intention to confirm that they have been received.
3.	Person B expresses any of his or her needs that are not met in the conflict.	Listens and reflects any observations, feelings, needs and wishes that Person B expresses.
4.	Person A reflects the needs Person B expressed with or without the help of the mediator.	Supports Person A to reflect back the unmet needs of person B.
5.	A natural shift from conflict to connection and understanding. Cooperation to achieve a resolution that suits both parties. The parties start talking about strategies that can meet the needs of both sides.	Helps with getting to do-able specific strategies. If any of the previous steps are not clear the mediator can lead the parties back. Provides empathy to restore the connection between the parties if needed.

Mediation step by step

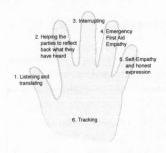

The five steps shown in the chart on the previous page make up a theoretical map that gives you an overview of what can happen during a mediation process. The chart may make mediation look like a linear process where we can always predict what step comes next. This is not the case since mediation is much more unpredictable than any model can describe. The chart can still be useful as a framework that provides guidance and support. Remember to first and foremost put your attention on creating connection between the parties. Be prepared to jump between the different steps when unexpected things happen.

It may provide the parties with some extra clarity to see this chart before they enter a mediation.

Practicing formal mediation - in slow motion

You have previously had a chance to practice a variety of tools that can be used in mediation. Maybe it is not yet totally clear to you how mediation works. In addition, maybe you don't have courage enough to try out your skills in real life. If this is the case, then this exercise is the next step for you. It can be done both individually and in a small group. In this exercise you will get a chance to listen to different expressions from one of the parties in a relaxed tempo. You will also practice dealing with everything that is expressed and explore how the situation shifts depending on how people are treated. The exercise will probably not give you the experience of an entire mediation situation because this may take more time than you want to use.

If you do the exercise in a group, one person can take on the role of Person A, one person takes the role of Person B, and the rest are mediators. Using these roles may make it easier to imagine what the different parties might express.

Start by choosing a situation. It may be a real situation, something you have heard, or something just made up. When many people do the exercise together, it may be helpful to have a flip chart or a large paper to write down the dialogue on.

You can practice giving the fictional parties some brief information about how you would like to work during the mediation or just start with the lines below and deal with whatever comes up.

Use the chart "Mediation in five steps" on the previous page, as well as "Reminders for the mediator", as support during the exercise.

Two people have asked you to mediate between them. Person A says:

> *"I think it's a stupid idea to launch a new project now that we have finally started to get things going."*

Person B responds:

> *"It's exactly this kind of attitude that makes me so mad at you. You are always so afraid of everything."*

a) Write down what you would say to mediate between them.

b) Write down what Person A or B says when they hear this.

c) Write down what you would say then.

Continue for as long as it feels meaningful. If you want to raise the bar, you can, for example, let Person B start talking while Person A is expressing himself or herself. This way, you get a chance to practice interrupting and possibly also giving first-aid empathy. Take turns suggesting what the mediator and the parties might say.

Chapter 9

Challenges and opportunities

Variations of mediation

Because mediation is a living process, it is very useful to follow your intuition and not get caught up in how mediation should work or how the order of things should progress. Every mediation is unique. Your task is to make the process smoother. If you don't believe that what you are doing will lead to more connection and cooperation, you can address this and suggest other ways to move forward. Here are some examples of how mediation can be varied.

1. When neither party wants to listen

As a mediator, you can obviously only listen to one person at a time. Sometimes a mediation is so intense that both parties want to express themselves, but neither of them wants to listen. In these situations, try expressing yourself along these lines:

"As I understand it, you both want to be heard. At the same time you are saying that you don't want to hear more from person B right now. I really want to be of help to you in this situation, but I can only listen to one at a time. Now that you have heard this, I wonder if anyone wants to try and listen to the other person for a while?"

Wait a brief moment and see if anything changes for anyone. If it doesn't, decide together whether you want to continue in some other way. See paragraphs 2-5 for more ideas.

You can also be proactive by, for example, interrupting someone who takes more time to express themselves than you guess the other person is able to take and say:

"I'm worried that this is taking longer than person B can handle, so I want to get a bit more connection with him before you say more. Is that OK?"

Remember that you only want a brief moment of connection with person B and not start a new cycle or process. There is a risk that you will do this if you ask an open question of person B such as:

"What are you feeling right now?"

Try saying something like this instead:

"I'd like to listen to person A for a little while so that I understand what she wants to say, before I listen to you. Is it okay for you to wait?"

If person B answers:

"No, it's not okay for me to listen any longer,"

and person A doesn't want to make the shift to listen to person B, you can try some of the options described in the following paragraphs.

2. In different rooms

If the mediation talk takes place between two people who turn out having a very difficult time connecting and hearing each other, it can help a lot if there are two mediators. In this way you can change your method of working and the two mediators listen to one person each, in different locations. This takes the pressure off the participants when they don't need to listen and understand the other person while needing to be heard and understood themselves.

Being the only mediator, you can of course still listen to the parties individually, though it takes longer. You can suggest this by saying:

"I am a bit worried because I want to help you and I don't trust that I am doing that right now. Therefore, I would like to take a break and then use x amount of time (e.g. 20 minutes) to listen to each of you alone. Only after that would I like to determine if we shall continue the talk with all three of us together. Do you have anything against that?"

The next step is to bring them together again and help them to hear each other or to find another way to move forward.

One of the first times I was invited to act as a third party, I was quite tense and nervous. It was in a conflict between two colleagues and both were angry about things that had recently happened in their collaboration.

They were both very passionate about their work and because they valued different things, the situation had gotten pretty heated. Since I really wanted to contribute (and also to be seen as very capable), I was not as attentive as I would have liked to have been. As a result, I continued the mediation talk with the parties in the same room even when this was no longer productive.

The mediation started to get constructive only when I, after having swallowed my unproductive pride, suggested that I would listen to each party in separate rooms. Afterwards, they were more willing to listen to each other with the intention of understanding each other's differences.

Later on, when I thought about how it was that I had not proposed this approach earlier, I realized several things. I realized that I had a strong idea about what a good mediation looks like, and that it is better not to separate the parties and listen to them individually. Believing this to be true, I interpreted the mediation as a failure. When I wasn't connected with my need to be seen, it unconsciously ruled over me and made it more difficult for me to see what contributed most to the parties. In any case, I got a much-needed lesson about not hesitating to take a break, and about the importance of proposing a different approach or even the possibility of breaking up the mediation.

3. Communication through the mediator

When the mediator asks the parties to turn directly towards each other and express what they need, it can sometimes be perceived as a demand; that they must understand each other. If the parties experience the meditation talk as something coercive, it is easy for them to become defensive - which can be a barrier for connection between them. This is what is going on when, for example, one party is engaged in preparing what he or she is going to say while the other party is talking, instead of really trying to listen and understand.

In some situations it may be experienced as less of a demand if the party who is talking turns directly to the mediator. Now the parties can concentrate on listening to each other without falling victim to thoughts like "I must be able to rephrase what has been said". This can remove unnecessary pressure that may be in the way of each person seeing how they can help each other meet their needs.

There are some disadvantages to having all communication go through the mediator. For example, I have found that the parties sometimes feel that the mediator, through his or her connection with the other party, is taking sides. Moreover, it can sometimes take longer to establish a connection between the parties if everything goes through the mediator.

Remember to choose your approach depending on the parties' ability to be present and to hear each other, as well as their understanding of conflict management.

This approach is somewhat different from those which we have touched upon earlier. I suggest that you as a mediator try to decide from situation to situation which approach can meet the most needs. You can invite the parties to work in the way described above by saying something like:

"I would really like to be a support for you both in understanding each other. Therefore, I suggest that you talk directly to me rather than to each other. My intention is that you both will be heard fully and I think this way will make it easier. Do you mind if we do so for a while and then evaluate how it is working?"

If you agree to move forward in this way and the person who is talking still turns towards the other person, you can interrupt that person and ask him or her to talk directly to you. In this way of working, you are not asking the other person to rephrase feelings and needs as this may be experienced as pressuring and difficult. Reflect the needs that you have heard one of the parties express to you. Even though the parties are just listening without rephrasing each other's needs, this helps to create more understanding and connection between them.

4a. The mediator takes one of the roles

Sometimes a person may have such strong inner processes that he or she has great difficulties to, for example, reflect back what the other person is saying. If you for some reason hesitate to listen to the parties separately, there are also other options.

One option is that you take the role of one of the parties while the person sits quietly, listening and observing. In this role you approach the other with empathy, and express yourself in the role of the person you are playing. It is essential that you express yourself without analysis, threats, demands or judgments in this role.

During a mediation between a married couple we all decided, after some ineffective attempts to establish connection, that I would role-play the husband. I took on the role, first listening to the wife. She had held back until that point, not daring to be honest for fear that her husband wouldn't be able to hear what she wanted to say. When she felt freer to express herself and not constantly worrying about not being heard, it soon became clear what she needed and wanted.

We continued with the wife listening to the husband's feelings and needs, with me still taking the role of the husband. I expressed what I had heard him say earlier. Instead of doing so in the form of criticism and demands, I expressed the longing and the needs that were behind the demands and the criticism. It was easy for the wife to hear what he needed when it was expressed in this form, so we quickly reached a solution. When I stepped out of the role and asked the husband how it had been for him to listen and if the solution was agreeable for him, he exclaimed:

"You know me better than I know myself!"

He hadn't understood what it was that he needed until now. In addition, he was very happy with the solution we had arrived at because it also met his needs.

4b. Two mediators each take a role

If there are two mediators and the mediation talk doesn't develop as you would like, another variation is for each of you to take one role. Then you show how you can talk about the core of the conflict in a way that creates connection. Just as in paragraph 4a, it is of course important to get back to the parties and ask if they recognize themselves in the role play and see how they can benefit from it.

5. Record the talks

An alternative to dealing with situations where it is difficult for the parties to meet, is to meet with them separately. Record a conversation where you take on the role of the other party; listening and expressing needs as in paragraph 4. Afterwards you meet with the other party who then can listen to the recorded dialogue.

When he or she has listened to the recording, you take the role of the other person, make a recording, and let he or she listen. After having done this a few times there may be enough understanding to have a mediation talk with both parties present at the same time.

The steps for doing this can look like this:

Step 1: The dialogue between person A and the mediator in the role of person B is recorded. Person A shares what he or she wants person B to hear and the mediator listens with empathy and expresses what person B might feel and need.

Step 2: The mediator meets with person B who listens to the recording from step 1. The mediator then answers any questions and takes the role of person A in the same way as above. The dialogue is recorded.

Step 3: The mediator meets with person A who listens to the dialogue. The mediator responds to any questions and then you decide if you want to record yet another dialogue.

Step 4: Continue to make recordings as long as it is meaningful. Also keep evaluating whether you want to continue in this form or if you want to try a mediation where both parties are present with the mediator at the same time.

Even if one party does not want to talk with a mediator, listening to a recording of a conversation can make a difference in the connection between the parties. First, a recording is made of a conversation where the other has met you as a mediator and where you take on the role of the party who is not present. Then the party who does not want to participate gets a chance to listen to what has been recorded. On several occasions, I have experienced that this has opened up a dialogue between the parties, with or without a third party.

6. Threatening situations

If you are worried that the situation might be intimidating for someone, you can ask an additional person to be present at the mediation for added safety. When the parties are very upset you can choose to hear them separately. Read more about this in the section "Shuttle mediation".

If you think the presence of another person will create more tension, it is important to be open about what the purpose is of having him or her there and to ask those involved if they object against having another person there.

In some cases it may also be counter-productive to have the parties meet before the mediation. Such is the case if there is suspicion about threats that would make it difficult for the involved parties to be honest and open.

One of the principles of Nonviolent Communication deals with using power as a protective force. We can use this principle as support to intervene when someone's health or life is in danger. If we use physical strength to control someone else we do it to protect others and not to punish the person who might be using violence.

This also applies to situations where we use the power we may have in an authority position. Read more about this in chapter 10 under the title "Intervening to protect rather than to punish". This section deals with the protective use of power in relation to children.

7. The mediator as a fellow human

Whenever you as a mediator sense that it may help, you can be more active in the dialogue by expressing your own feelings, needs and requests. To share how you are affected as a third party when you listen to what the parties are expressing can generate a new angle on an issue where they have gotten stuck. It can also generate new and creative ways to handle things. If you show your humanity, you can also serve as a model for the parties to express their vulnerability and willingness to be open and honest.

I once mediated between two groups on Sri Lanka. They worked together in a project which I experienced as a very meaningful and important contribution to peace on this beautiful, but war-torn island. I really looked forward to being of help, and so I was extremely enthusiastic at the beginning of the mediation. However, when I heard about the amount of questions they could not agree upon, I gradually started to feel more and more powerless. We tried and tried "by the book", but got nowhere.

Finally, I did not want to hold back my despair any longer, and began to cry, expressing how sad I was. I shared that I wanted to find more ways to contribute to how they could agree with each other. I also expressed the pain I was feeling in seeing how difficult it was for them to manage their conflict.

After their surprise over my tears had subsided, this became a turning point. Several of them who had previously pointed out mostly what others had done wrong or should do differently, now began to share more about how they felt and what they longed for. This made it easier for others to listen. We could then come up with some specific things to move forward with.

When we summarized what we had agreed on, one person said:

"When I saw how desperate you were, I realized how important it is for me to help people feel good. It made me more willing to listen to the other party."

Before you express your own feelings and needs as a mediator, it can be useful to silently listen to yourself with empathy. Self-empathy helps you to reach beyond your own judgments and demands and find what needs of yours are stirred up. When you are connected to what you need, it is often a gift to express it.

The mediator's responsibility

The parties are responsible for their connection with each other, but this can be easily forgotten in the moment. As a mediator, you can therefore remind the parties of their responsibility when you sense that this might create connection.

During a mediation between a couple that I previously was familiar with, they quickly fell into their usual way of talking, which made connection difficult. They used a jargon of judgments, vague requests, hints of what one should expect from one's partner and so on. I tried to help in every way I could come up with: I translated judgments, interrupted and guessed what was going on within them. I "pulled them by the ear" and asked them to reflect back on what the other had said.

When nothing seemed to work, I got more and more worried, but also tiresome. I realized that my feelings were connected to my longing to make a difference and contribute to their relationship. After having connected with what was going on inside of me, I expressed myself something like this:

"I notice that I am a bit tiresome, but also worried because I want us all to put our energy into what may be valuable for our connection. I really want to contribute, but I am beginning to doubt whether you really want to create connection. To determine whether I can be of any real help to you, I want to hear something from both of you about how you want to contribute to your connection. Are you willing to say something about this?"

Since they had a very different picture of what I would say and do as a mediator, they were both very surprised to hear my honesty and there was a long silence. When they started to talk again, it was with a completely different tone and attitude than before.

At the end of the mediation, we talked about how they had experienced the mediation. They both said that when I expressed my worry and boredom they had discovered that they had handed over the responsibility for managing the conflict to me. It became clear to them that even if they could get support from an outside party, how they related and communicated was their shared responsibility.

I suggest that you intervene in this way and talk about what is going on inside of you after you have given yourself empathy. Your honesty has maximum effect if you express yourself after having translated any judgments or demands you have of those you are mediating between.

Situations where mediation might not be a good idea

When people are exposed to high levels of external or internal stress, a mediation talk where all parties are present at the same time is sometimes counterproductive. During this kind of mental overload, mediation can be completely unsuitable. Although not an easy thing to determine, it is up to each mediator to decide with each mediation talk.

Mediation between parties under the influence of alcohol and/or other drugs is not recommended. However, if we picture the role of the mediator as a facilitator of communication, some form of mediation is usually possible. It might help to be reminded that there are several variations of mediation. At the same time, keep in mind that the actual mediation talk needs to be part of a longer process if it is to have maximum effect, not just a separate event.

Process or separate event - shuttle mediation

Engaging in a dialogue with the parties before a mediation talk often takes more time and energy than the mediation itself. However, this process is just as important as the mediation talk.

It is easy to see mediation as a separate event. When we do this, we probably fail to see that mediation is only one link in a long chain of interactions and events. These links are present both before and after the mediation. When we stop seeing mediation as an isolated event, and instead see it as part of a process, we are more likely to release some of the pressure from the mediation talk. We can see more clearly that even if we do not arrive at a solution or an agreement during the mediation, the talk is a small but important part in a larger process that starts before the mediation and continues long after the mediation.

One way to prepare the parties before a mediation dialogue is to use "shuttle mediation". This means that the mediator meets with both parties separately with the purpose of creating a dialogue. This process can take much time and energy, but is sometimes the only way that the parties are willing to communicate together. This process has many advantages, for example it can help the parties get clear about what they want from the mediation.

On the next page you will find a structured exercise that illustrates what this type of dialogue looks like. Remember that these conversations can be far more informal than they might appear in the exercise. Shuttle mediation can be used for a number of reasons when there is a strong resistance between the two parties to communicate directly with each other. This process can build trust towards the other party. It is very important in this process that no information is communicated to the other party without consent from the first party. This becomes a way for the parties to talk about the problem and to get a chance to see it from different angles without having to deal with each other's reactions at the moment. Shuttle mediation may give the mediator important information in identifying the core of the conflict. Shuttle mediation can help us to see what kind of openings towards a mediation there may be between the parties, especially if the conflict concerns a number of parties. One of the participants in a mediation training I held in Thailand tried this out in a very hot situation after the training. She wrote:

"In one incident, a friend and I were in the middle of a conflict between a group of the anti-government protesters and a group of soldiers who were holding rifles in postures ready to shoot. We ran between the two sides and helped them communicate with each other. Finally, the problem was solved peacefully and no one was injured. I used mediation skills at my best efforts to save not only other people's lives but also mine."
Pairin Jotisakulratana, Peace activist, Thailand.

The purpose of a shuttle mediation

1. To create connection and trust in the process and the mediator.

2. To help the parties share their opinions and speak about what is painful for them in a safe way.

3. To clarify that the mediator is willing to listen to all sides.

4. To obtain sufficient information and transparency in order to determine when a mediation talk could take place.

5. To give the parties enough empathy and information so that they can open up to hear the other side.

6. To give the mediator a chance to clarify how mediation works.

7. To give the parties a chance to ask about how mediation works.

Shuttle mediation – preparations

1. Choose which parties you want to talk with first as a first step towards getting to a mediation.

2. Prepare yourself. Especially do inner work, for example, translate enemy images of the parties or of yourself.

3. Start by meeting one of the parties. Choose randomly, or use one of the following criteria for selecting which party to start with:

- Start with the one you think is most hesitant about a mediation talk.

- Start with the one you have the most difficulties in connecting with.

- Start with the one you previously have had the least amount of dialogue with.

4. Your main questions to Party A (the one you first talk with) are: "What would you need in order to say yes to meeting with Party B in a mediation?

Or

"Would you have anything against meeting with Party B, with me as a third party?"

Or

"I have confidence that it would make a difference if you/your party and Party B would meet with each other with me as a third party. What would you need in order to say yes to this?"

And

"Is there anything you want me to tell Party B when I meet with them? Or that you wish that they could hear or that you want their response on?

There can also be, of course, a Party C, D, E and so on. In this case, just proceed in the same way.

Exercise in shuttle mediation

The purpose of this exercise is to get a feel for what a shuttle mediation can look like. Practicing shuttle mediation can give insights into the challenges and opportunities of this type of mediation. Read through the text above about shuttle mediation before starting the exercise.

Roles

Party A = The person or group that you choose to begin talking with.
Party B = The person or group that you choose to talk with after having talked with Party A.
Mediator = Can be one or more persons who together help the parties to create a dialogue.

1. People might want some time to talk about how they want to act in their assigned roles. If there is more than one mediator, it can be useful to spend some time together to think about how they want to cooperate. Take about 10 minutes.

2. The mediator/mediators meet with Party A for approximately 10 minutes. If you have gained clarity before the time is up you can break and proceed with Party B.

3. Give Party B 10 minutes to answer the same question. Pass along any messages from Party A.

4. Meet with Party A again.

5. Meet with Party B again.

6. This continues until you have reached the end of the agreed upon time for the exercise or until both parties have agreed to have a mediation talk together.

This exercise can be varied in many ways. For example, you can change the amount of time with each party, let everyone switch roles, try role playing with two mediators and let the parties be fairly large groups or end with a mediation talk where all the parties meet.

It's not about doing "the right thing"

I'm grateful for the following story written by Terry Dobson. It shows that if we want to relate to people who are upset, it's not about doing what is "right" nor is it about following any particular method. This story shows a true desire to create connection and to see the humanity in a person who threatens or frightens others.

To me, it also shows clearly how tempting it can be to try to win over someone. It shows how dangerous the idea of "the strongest wins" is in certain situations.

The train clanked and rattled through the suburbs of Tokyo on a drowsy spring afternoon. Our car was comparatively empty – a few housewives with their kids in tow, some old folks going shopping. I gazed absently at the drab houses and dusty hedgerows.

At one station the doors opened, and suddenly the afternoon quiet was shattered by a man bellowing violent, incomprehensible curses. The man staggered into our car. He wore laborer's clothing, and he was big, drunk, and dirty. Screaming, he swung at a woman holding a baby. The blow sent her spinning into the laps of an elderly couple. It was a miracle that the baby was unharmed.

Terrified, the couple jumped up and scrambled toward the other end of the car. The labourer aimed a kick at the retreating back of the old woman but missed as she scuttled to safety. This so enraged the drunk that he grabbed the metal pole in the center of the car and tried to Wrench it out of its stanchion. I could see that one of his hands was cut and bleeding. The train lurched ahead, the passengers frozen with fear. I stood up.

I was a young man then, some twenty years ago, and in a pretty good shape. I'd been putting in a solid eight hours of Aikido training nearly every day for the past three years. I liked to throw and grapple. I thought I was tough. The trouble was, my martial skill was untested in actual combat. As students of Aikido, we were not allowed to fight.

"Aikido", my teacher had said again and again, "is the art of reconciliation. Whoever has the mind to fight has broken his connection with the universe. If you try to dominate people, you are already defeated. We study how to resolve conflict, not how to start it."

I listened to his words. I tried hard. I even went so far as to cross the street

A Helping Hand
Mediation with Nonviolent Communication

to avoid the chimpira, the pinball punks who lounged around the train stations. My forbearance exalted me. I felt both tough and holy. In my heart, however, I wanted an absolutely legitimate opportunity whereby I might save the innocent by destroying the guilty.

"This is it!" I said to myself as I got to my feet. "People are in danger. If I don't do something fast, somebody will probably get hurt."

Seeing me stand up, the drunk recognized a chance to focus his rage. "Aha!" He roared. "A foreigner! You need a lesson in Japanese manners!"

I held on lightly to the commuter strap overhead and gave him a slow look of disgust and dismissal. I planned to take this turkey apart, but he had to make the first move. I wanted him mad, so I pursed my lips and blew him an insolent kiss.

"All right!" He hollered. "You're gonna get a lesson." He gathered himself for a rush at me.

A fraction of a second before he could move, someone shouted "Hey!" It was earsplitting. I remember the strangely joyous, lilting quality of it – as though you and a friend had been searching diligently for something, and he had suddenly stumbled upon it. "Hey!"

I wheeled to my left; the drunk spun to his right. We both stared down at a little, old Japanese man. He must have been well into his seventies, this tiny gentleman, sitting there immaculate in his kimono. He took no notice of me, but beamed delightedly at the labourer, as though he had a most important, most welcome secret to share.

"C'mere," the old man said in an easy vernacular, beckoning to the drunk. "C'mere and talk with me." He waved his hand lightly.

The big man followed, as if on a string. He planted his feet belligerently in front of the old gentleman, and roared above the clacking wheels, "Why the hell should I talk to you?" The drunk now had his back to me. If his elbow moved so much as a millimeter, I'd drop him in his socks.

The old man continued to beam at the labourer. "What'cha been drinkin'?" he asked, his eyes sparkling with interest. "I been drinking sake" the labourer bellowed back, "and it's none of your business!" Flecks of spittle spattered the old man.

"Oh, that's wonderful," the old man said, "absolutely wonderful! You see, I love sake too. Every evening, me and my wife (she's seventy-six, you know), we warm up a little bottle of sake and take it out in the garden, and we sit on the old wooden bench. We watch the sun go down, and we look to see how *the persimmon tree is doing. My great-grandfather planted that tree, and we worry about whether it will recover from those ice storms we had last winter. Our tree has done better than I expected, though, especially when you consider the poor quality of the soil. It is gratifying to watch when we take our sake and go out to enjoy the evening – even when it rains!" He looked up at the labourer, eyes twinkling.*

As he struggled to follow the old man's conversation, the drunk's face began to soften. His fists slowly unclenched. "Yeah," he said. "I love persimmons, too..." His voice trailed off.

"Yes," said the old man, smiling, "and I'm sure you have a wonderful wife."

"No," replied the labourer. "My wife died." Very gently, swaying with the motion of the train, the big man began to sob. "I don't got no wife, I don't got no home, I don't got no job. I'm so ashamed of myself." Tears rolled down his cheeks; a spasm of despair rippling through his body.

Now it was my turn. Standing there in my well-scrubbed youthful innocence, my make-this-world-safe-for-democracy righteousness, I suddenly felt dirtier than he was.

Then the train arrived at my stop. As the doors opened, I heard the old man cluck sympathetically. "My, my," he said, "that is a difficult predicament, indeed. Sit down here and tell me about it."

I turned my head for one last look. The labourer was sprawled out on the seat, his head in the old man's lap. The old man was softly stroking the filthy, matted hair. As the train pulled away, I sat down on a bench. What I had wanted to do with muscle had been accomplished with kind words. I had just seen Aikido tried in combat, and the essence of it was love. I would have to practice the art with an entirely different spirit. It would be a long time before I could speak about the resolution of conflict.

Terry Dobson[1]

I love the way Uyeshiba Morihei describes what Aikido is about. I find these principles very useful in mediation.

The secret of Aikido is to harmonize ourselves with the movement of the universe and bring ourselves into accord with the universe itself. He who has gained the secret of Aikido has the universe in himself and can say, "I am the universe."

---

1 Dass & Gorman (1997), Handbok för hjälpare. Natur och kultur

A Helping Hand
Mediation with Nonviolent Communication

When an enemy tries to fight with me, the universe itself, he has to break the harmony of the universe. Hence, at the moment he has the mind to fight with me, he is already defeated.
Winning means winning over the mind of discord in yourself.... . Then how can you straighten your Warped mind, purify your heart, and be harmonized with the activities of all things in nature? You should first make God's heart yours. It is a Great Love Omnipresent in all quarters and in all times of the universe. "There is no discord in love. There is no enemy on Love."
Uyeshiba Morihei (Founder of Aikido)[1]

Our choices will affect others

A teenage boy who was caught after having snatched a purse from an old lady was invited to be part of a mediation, but at first he did not at all understand what the point of it was.

There were a lot of things going on in him. He felt frustrated with all the adults who thought he was annoying and who wanted him to realize that he shouldn't have done what he did. He also felt guilt and shame because he too thought he had done something wrong. He felt that he had hit a low water mark and that he wasn't worth a second chance. All these feelings mixed together with the thoughts that were the source of them, made it difficult for him to say yes to participation in a mediation. The thought of hearing even more said about him being a thief and that he should have known better made the mediation talk seem very unappealing.

He finally said yes when he realized that a mediation could be valuable for the woman who's bag he had snatched.

Present at the mediation was the boy, the boy's parents, the woman, the woman's closest friend and the mediator. During the mediation, the boy slumped down in his chair as it dawned on him just how his actions had affected the woman. With tears in his eyes he listened to the woman and her friend when they expressed how scared they had become about going out, after what had happened. After a while, tears ran down his cheeks when he listened as the women described how rarely they dared to visit each other nowadays.

I believe that when the boy really took in how he had affected someone

---

1 http://en.wikipedia.org/wiki/Morihei_Ueshiba, 11 july 2008.

else's way of life in this way, it contributed to his willingness to be involved in repairing what had happened. I am convinced that the insight about how his actions affected others, affected him in a completely different way than if he had only received an "ordinary" punishment. It also had a different impact on him than if he had apologized, perhaps under the threat of punishment if he didn't. Now, he had the opportunity to participate in repairing the consequences of his actions.

They agreed that he would follow the woman and her friend during their visits about two to three times each week over a period of time.

This gave him an opportunity to restore his self-respect.

For people who have committed a crime, to restore one's self-respect is one of the most valuable aspects of mediation in a judicial matter. It is more likely that people with low self-respect will commit new crimes if they do not value their own life very highly. When you see yourself as important, you begin caring about how you act and about the consequences of your actions.

Moral development

What motivates us to do or not to do things is based on our moral development. There is much we could say about this, but I would like to summarize a few brief points inspired by psychologist Lawrence Kohlberg's theories about moral stages. I believe that we can create a lasting peaceful society only when the motivation to act with care for others comes from within.

"I don't do this because it is forbidden."
The motivation is to follow established laws.

"I don't do this because I may get punished if anyone catches me doing it."
The motivation is to escape punishment.

"I don't do this because then others won't like me."
The motivation is to be liked by others; to "buy love".

"I don't do this because I see that it can harm others."
The motivation comes from within, as I see how my actions might harm others and because mutual respect and care are important to me.

Mediation in crime

Mediation in crime is based on the idea that when a crime has been committed, those affected by the crime benefit from being part of an attempt to repair the damage. Unlike the current justice system which is based on thinking in terms of punishment, mediation in crime focuses on the needs that have not been met for those who have been affected. Mediation can give people a chance to experience healing and reconciliation. Also, those who have committed a crime can be helped to take responsibility for their actions, instead of only serving a sentence.

When a person who has committed a crime is part of a mediation, he or she is given the opportunity to hear how his or her actions have affected others. This can lead to change on a deep level, through really taking in, and reflecting on, these questions:

"After hearing how the other person's life has been affected by what you have done, how do you feel?"
And

"What can you do to completely or at least partially repair what has happened?"

In some cases, a contract can be created between the parties. It may concern following guidelines during the mediation, and what can be done if these guidelines are not followed. When you as a mediator notice that agreements are not being followed, you can address this. You can, for example, ask if anyone is opposed to continuing, or if the parties no longer have the intention to create connection and to be part of repairing what has happened.

If for some reason the parties lose connection with their intention, it is important to either cancel the mediation or, with the help of empathic listening, try to create understanding about what is going on.

As of 2008, people in Sweden under 21 years of age, who have committed a crime are offered the possibility of mediation. In some cases, it is also offered to people older than 21. Mediation is an addition to the ordinary judicial process. The hope is that this will give all those involved a clearer sense of what the most common offenses among young people (assault, theft, illegal threats, vandalism and shoplifting) can lead to for the victims. The purpose of the mediation is to reduce the negative consequences for both perpetrators and victims.

This approach gives me great hope, as I believe that when we realize that we are not only doing something against the law, but also doing something against other people, we will be more likely to change our behavior. If we deeply understand how we have impacted on other people, the motivation to act with greater care becomes greater than when the motivation is solely to follow the law. I have confidence that if we, instead of focusing on punishing those who have committed crimes, focus on repairing what can be repaired, our ability to prevent further crime will increase.

Various agreements can be made during a mediation. It can, for example, include how the parties want to treat each other in the future.

Although most principles and skills described in this book can be used for mediation in crime, there are additional aspects to consider than are covered here.

Summary -
What mediation in crime can contribute to:

- Preventing new crimes.

- Giving the victim an opportunity to get answers to their questions and show how the crime has affected them.

- Conflict resolution.

- An educational impact – demonstrating another way of managing conflicts.

- An opportunity for the offender to experience self-respect.

- Support for the offender in reshaping his/her self-image as a "criminal".

- Participation. Several parties are given a chance to participate in dealing with the crime from more than a judicial standpoint.

- To alleviate from the existing legal system less serious crimes that can be resolved between the parties.

Restorative justice

Mediation in crime is based on the philosophy of restorative justice. Restorative justice is a relatively new concept within traditional criminology. It can be described as an alternative way of relating to the consequences of a crime and how to repair the damage of an assault.

The principles themselves are ancient and have been used in different cultures worldwide. The idea is to give the victim an opportunity to tell the offender how the crime has affected them and their everyday life, thereby creating an opportunity for healing.

One aim of restorative justice is to be both crime preventive and healing. For this to happen, the offender needs to be seen as part of a social context. Without seeing the offender as somebody who has a clear link to the society people live in, mediation in crime risks losing its crime preventive aspect. For example, follow-up meetings are sometimes left out due to a mistaken concern for efficiency.

When follow-up meetings are dropped on account of efficiency and cost, chances are that we actually end up in the long run with lower efficiency and increased costs. We miss making use of the force of social change that mediation has the potential to be.

Restorative justice is in contrast to the traditional legal system that is practiced daily in most countries around the world. This system basically means that the State and the offender meet during which a given framework is followed, and punishment is set on a pre-determined scale. If we use mediation in crime while at the same time seeing one person as the guilty party, we miss the possibility of seeing where major changes need to happen. We are now supporting a mediation between an offender and a victim, but forget to see the offender as part of a context that has contributed to, or failed to prevent, the crime.

Restorative justice is based on ancient knowledge of what needs to be done in a society when someone has made a mistake. For example, the Maoris have used councils for this over millennia. In these councils, the offender and victim are not the only ones participating in a mediation. Families of both parties, friends and others surrounding the parties may be invited to join. Everyone is given a chance to express themselves, to give support and to point out how things are related to each other.

As I see it, we all make mistakes. It is when we make mistakes that we need support the most from our fellow human beings.

Howard Zehr, an advocate of restorative justice, has compared some questions that illustrate typical differences between the traditional legal system and the restorative way of thinking:

Traditional legal system:

Which laws have been broken?
Who did it?
What kind of punishment do they deserve?

Restorative system:

Who has been hurt?
What are their needs?
What is needed to repair this?

In our legal system, punishment is intended to show that a law has been broken. How a crime has affected someone is rarely considered. Victims of crime seldom have a say in what punishments is meted out nor are asked as to how they were affected by the crime. In contrast, the victim's needs are the focus of restorative justice. Great emphasis is placed on the offender's responsibility to help repair the damage that he or she has caused.

Summary of Restorative justice

Focus on:

- Repairing rather than punishing.

- The offender and the victim, not on the legal system.

- The offender understanding consequences and taking responsibility.

- Active participation on behalf of the victim.

- Reconciliation and integration.

Mediation in the work place

I sometimes say, half seriously and half jokingly, "if only we were as smart as horses, we would find ways to cooperate much quicker". This thought is based on observations I made during the annual "release of the stallions" which I visited in my teenage years. Every spring, young stallions are released on the large meadows outside the town where I live. Lots of people gather at this event, excited to watch the horses create a hierarchy among themselves. At first, there are large clashes which include both biting and kicking. But by dusk the ranking is complete and the horses graze peacefully together. If we could come together as quickly as horses, our workgroups would be much more effective in reaching their common goals.

Of course I don't suggest that we bite and kick each other. We need another form of communication that works for us humans. I believe that we would have greater cooperation if we would more clearly express what we want, dare to be vulnerable and "put all our cards on the table".

What is it that so many times makes it more difficult for humans to find a structure for cooperation? How come most people can report that they have, on some occasion, been in a workgroup where recurring conflicts have drained everyone's energy? Were we once just as naturally skilled in creating a well functioning group as horses are? Are there people and groups that still have this capacity to cooperate with ease and effectiveness?

There are no simple answers to these questions. I believe that our challenges are partly the result of a tendency to place high importance in who the leader is. We rank ourselves in a hierarchical way, even when it is not functional. To work in a hierarchical structure or to blindly follow authority is not the solution. We need to find a way of relating that truly serves all who are part of a group, and is applicable for us humans. And the way we choose needs to harmonize with nature and other living beings in mutual respect.

In a domination system the leader's position is seen as the most important of all the social functions or roles. In most organizations the leaders have the highest salary and the most benefits. They are seen as deserving extra benefits and greater prosperity than others. It isn't surprising that people in these systems fight to be the leader in a group or try to obstruct others from becoming leaders. Since we have learned the importance of rewards outside ourselves, of winning and of ownership, these are the strategies that we often pursue.

Because leadership is often so charged, we sometimes miss that there are also positive effects in this system. As a result, we have difficulties creating well functioning groups that also support the leader. Because we also have learned to be motivated by outer rewards, it is important to be friendly towards the leader, since the leader is the one with the power to reward or punish. This leads to people hiding things that threaten the system, instead of "putting their cards on the table". Everything that we try to avoid dealing with runs the risk of growing into conflicts that later explode and become difficult to manage.

In such systems, it is quite common that people who long for something new try to commit mutiny, or lead from the back. This can create further situations of conflict. How do these kinds of power struggles affect a mediation within a group? Imagine a conversation in a work group where most of the group process takes place below the surface:

Sarah: "Michael wants blue wallpaper in the staff room!"

Emily: "I've always said that I don't think it will look good in blue. I definitely want to go with green."

Sarah: "David seems to agree with blue."

Emily: "Oh... Well, blue might not be such a bad idea, if it is in the right tone."

This is a common and often unconscious way of acting in a group when we are searching for hierarchy and control. When you as a mediator work in groups, be prepared to deal with "old stuff" that you, in the beginning, may not understand at all. Everything that hasn't previously been dealt with can affect the conflicts that exist today. Because of this it can be difficult to understand why the color of wallpaper can become so important that it takes months to come to any decision about it.

If it becomes clear to you that the conflict between Michael and Emily has persisted over a long period of time, you can see the situation in a new light. When you hear that the conflict has taken several forms, it can be easier to understand why focus is now on the color of the wallpaper, even though the core of the problem is something completely different. Still, don't belittle the positive impact it can have on a group if they can together find a solution to a seemingly insignificant thing. This can give them much-needed hope that they really can cooperate. This may be much more important than what it appears to be, especially if they have had difficult conflicts stretched over time. It can have a significant impact on the wellbeing of the entire group, even though everyone is fully aware that they haven't gotten to the core of the conflict yet or found a solution to all parts of it.

In the case above, Emily has strong ties to David who supports her. Therefore, she wants to make sure she doesn't do anything that might interfere with this relationship. In a group with many strong subgroups it can seem like everyone is open about a specific issue, where in fact things are primarily going on under the surface. Honesty can be perceived as a threat to the positions that have been built up, especially if the conflict itself is about influence and leadership. Since transparency is a prerequisite for a successful mediation, it may be necessary to spend some time and energy on creating the trust that team members need in order to have the courage to be honest.

It can be very challenging to mediate in a group with many areas of taboo, strong emphasis on competition and little ability to manage conflicts. To prevent conflicts, leaders can consciously organize groups in a way that does not promote competition but instead ensures that the focus is on cooperation and mutual respect. This will also minimize the number of conflicts. Leaders can create incentives for cooperation other than fear of punishment or promises of reward. Any action that facilitates participation, or provides opportunities to influence decisions that affect a large part of the group, will also help.

Moreover, groups that are willing to be open about areas of taboo such as money, conflicts, strong emotions such as anger or sadness, and want to learn from their mistakes, are more likely to manage conflicts in a satisfactory way. Such a group will also be more open to embracing the opportunity to ask a third party for support.

Appreciation - Conflict prevention

Throughout my 25 years as a consultant, trainer and mediator, I have frequently asked teams if they feel that they give and receive a satisfactory amount of gratitude. I have yet to get yes for an answer. Most of us long to hear more often that what we are doing actually makes a difference in a positive way for others. When we do not hear appreciation as much as we would like to hear, it is easy to believe that it is because others don't appreciate what we have done and we might easily just accept this.

But, honestly, how many people around you get to hear about all the appreciation and gratitude you feel for them? Most of us don't even come close to expressing as much gratitude as we experience. When I ask what stands in the way of expressing gratitude and appreciation, I usually get these two answers:

"She already knows how much I appreciate her!"

"But he doesn't listen. It seems like he just gets so bothered whenever he receives appreciation!"

Do you really want this to be the reason for not expressing what you appreciate? Do you think that people around you don't want to hear appreciation, even though they know that you appreciate things that they have done? Wouldn't they want to hear that you are grateful, even if they feel embarrassed and are unfamiliar with openly receiving gratitude?

Would you yourself like to hear more appreciation for the things you do? My guess is that the answer is yes. What does gratitude have to do with mediation? Inspired by something I have heard Marshall Rosenberg suggest, I have asked various working groups if they, as a test, would schedule time when they could talk about things they appreciate. Simply to talk about what works and what you appreciate about what others are doing. It can for example be during staff meetings, management team meetings or during an informal weekly coffee break. I have suggested that they use at least 10 minutes to do this. In the beginning, this sounds like a long time to many people. However, when I have met with them some time later, most have said that they now use at least 20 minutes, and that they really like it.

The result? Every group that has taken up this challenge has expressed how it simultaneously has become easier to manage conflicts and things that don't work. How can this be? I think when people recognize the great opportunity we have to contribute to others, they also see how much joy using this opportunity brings. When we are connected to this joy we will probably consciously want to enrich both our own and others' lives.

Also, to experience being part of a team where everyone is seen and where honesty is highly valued is very nourishing. There are strong driving forces to protect such a group community, for example by managing conflicts that may arise.

Appreciation à la NVC

To get maximum return on gratitude, it needs to be expressed in a way that really has a potential of contributing. If other people get to know exactly what they have said or done that we appreciate, it is easier for them to fully take in what we want to say. We need to express ourselves in the language of observations so that there is no mistaking what we mean.

The next step is to express how their actions have affected us. In what way have their words or actions made our life more enjoyable, comfortable and easier? How do we feel and which of our needs have been met by this?

Step 1. Express what you have seen the other person do or what you have heard them say. Be as specific as possible, quote if this is helpful.

Step 2. Express how this has enriched you; what you feel and which of your needs were met.

If I express myself in the form of praise or approval, saying who I think is good, clever or wonderful, there is a risk that this creates distance. This might especially happen if the other person doesn't know how to listen to and to absorb what I say. Instead of judging a person as "clever", you can say:

"I'm so relieved and really appreciate that you've done all this, because it makes my work much easier."

Instead of judging someone as "wonderful", you can say:

"I feel so happy when I think of the last five times we have worked together. I've had so much fun and I've learned a lot from your way of relating to people. Do you want to hear more?"

Gratitude expressed in this way gives back more energy to the person who hears it. It also clarifies in what way he or she has contributed. As for the person who expresses the gratitude, it provides a completely different feeling of celebration. It is very different to tell someone how you have been touched by what he or she has done, rather than to judge the person as "good" or "clever".

Daily nutrition

One way to develop as a mediator is to set aside some time each day to reflect on the past. Bring to mind something that you are grateful for having done, or something someone else has done. Stay conscious of the feelings that are stimulated in you when you do this. Connect what you are feeling with the needs that were met by that action. Reminding yourself of the power you and others have to enrich others can give you the courage to mediate when it is needed the most. The following story inspires me to see gratitude in a larger perspective.

> *The tribe I have had some contact with is Orang Asilie tribe in Malaysia. I'll never forget what my translator was saying before we got started. He was going over how he was going to translate. He pointed out that his language has no verb to be, like [you are] good, bad, wrong, right. You can't classify people if you take away the verb to be. How are you going to insult people? You take away ninety percent of my vocabulary! So I say what are you going to say if I say "You're selfish"?*
> *He responded, "It's going to be hard. I'd translate it like this: Marshall says he sees you are taking care of your needs but not the needs of others."*
> *He says, "In my language, you tell people what they are doing and what you like them to do differently, it would not occur to us to tell people what they are." He then paused and he looked at me in all sincerity and said, "Why would you ever call a person a name?"*
> *I said you have to know who to punish. Punishment is a totally foreign concept in these tribes and cultures. He looked at me and said, "If you*

have a plant and it isn't growing the way you would like, do you punish it?" The whole idea of punishment is so ingrained in us that it is hard for us to imagine other options. It is totally foreign to people who haven't been educated in culture of domination systems. In many of these cultures they look at people who hurt others this way: they are not bad, they've just forgotten their nature. They put them in a circle and they remind them of their true nature, what it's like to be real human beings. They've gotten alienated and they bring them back to life.

Conflict is costly

Is it possible to estimate how much a conflict costs? Human suffering is of course part of all conflicts and it can feel rather futile to talk about the economic aspect of this suffering. Still, here is an attempt to explore this matter.

Direct costs related to conflicts in workplaces are fairly easy to calculate. These include the cost of various experts who are hired to deal with the conflict: resource managers, occupational health people, mediators, consultants, therapists and lawyers, among others. Because invoices display information of the costs visually, you get very precise amounts.

Another more common cost is the much greater cost due to productivity decline. This isn't as visible as direct costs because there are more aspects that affect productivity. At a workplace with an ongoing conflict, each worker can spend an hour a day worrying about the conflict, being involved in various confrontations and then talking about the confrontations. An hour may sound like an exaggeration, but when the situation is at its worst one hour may be the lower end, when taking into account all aspects. When you sum up the loss of productivity, you get an estimate of the conflict's real cost. It is easy to see that a prolonged conflict can affect an organization's financial results. If you include loss of creativity, lower motivation and diminished cooperation, the costs increase even more.

A common reaction both during and after a conflict is that employees may quit. They do this not necessarily because they are disliked, but because they can't stand having so many relationships affected in a negative way. Organizations lose competency when employees quit. Furthermore, the cost of hiring and training new employees is huge.

A work place with a lot of conflicts leads to poorer mental health among employees, which can result in a lower frustration threshold and a higher level of stress. Such an environment is definitely not a good breeding ground for positive customer relationships, leading to inferior customer service. Disillusioned employees convey a poor image of the company. If we also add the other various forms of poor quality that tension among employees can bring about, there is a high risk that the company ends up with less satisfied customers. This in turn leads to even greater losses. These issues make it clear that the earlier conflicts are handled, the lower the costs.

Escalating or lowering conflicts

One way to describe how conflicts escalate is to imagine that conflicts exist on different levels. At the first level, both parties have the ability to remember both their own needs and the others' needs, as well as what the conflict is about. I'm upset, but it still is clear to me that I also want the other to be happy with how we resolve the conflict.

There are several reasons for an escalating conflict. A common reason is that the parties are not listening to each other and taking in each other's reality, or are unable to show the other that they do. Here, it is still clear that we want to manage the actual problem, but we don't think about how our actions will affect the other person. We may be acting out of fear that the other won't take our needs into account and we might not be satisfied with the outcome.

Just as common is the case where someone gives up on their own needs and interests, even though things don't feel okay. Here too, the conflict escalates. If, for example, there have been loud discussions, it can for this party become more important to experience harmony, acceptance, love and kindness than to stand up for their interests. Even the choice to give up when it is not voluntarily will often have unwanted consequences.

In relationships that extend over a long period of time, this can become a game where the greatest martyr "wins" at the price of closeness and trust.

Conflicts can escalate to a third level if the parties don't find ways to take each other's needs into account to a greater extent. At this point the problem isn't important any more. Now it is all about survival through, for example, revenge. Fortunately, it is rare that conflicts escalate to this level.

To prevent a conflict from escalating, at least one party or a third party needs to focus on everyone's needs. When the parties feel that everyone's needs are important, it is more likely that they will want to cooperate, thus lowering the conflict as a result.

Learn from your mistakes

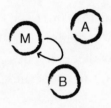

If you think that a mediation has failed, it is important that you find some way to cope with your disappointment. When we can approach our mistakes with a sense of curiosity about what we can learn, we create an opportunity for reflection on what has happened.

Thoughts about failure can make it difficult to find the motivation to mediate again. We worry that the same thing will happen again. Therefore, it is valuable to have efficient ways to mourn what has happened, learn from it, and find your motivation to try again.

In order to mourn mistakes in such a way that you can learn from them, the first step is to connect with the needs that were not met by something you did, or did not do, during the mediation. Take a moment to really connect with these needs. This can help you to clarify for yourself what you value and how to proceed.

The second step is to get in touch with the needs that you tried to meet. When this is clear to you, take some time to consider if there were other ways to meet those needs during the mediation.

The ability to quickly translate your own critical thoughts, both about yourself and others, is an invaluable tool for you as a mediator. You can practice this every day, whether you mediate or not. Evaluating how a mediation turned out is a way to continuously learn things about mediation. Therefore, take some time to do this often. If you want to maximize your learning, make sure that the evaluation is based on whether needs are met or not, rather than what you consider to be good or bad. You can use the questions on the next page to connect with your own needs. Remember that you can also use other people as a support to sort out what you did that did or did not meet your needs.

Evaluating your mediation skills

Use this evaluation after a mediation you aren't happy with, or that you would have liked to have done differently.

1. Start by writing down what you say to yourself about your contribution. Allow for any thoughts to come, including the most critical ones. The more you allow yourself to be honest about what you think, the more you can get out of the exercise. Do you have any judgments about yourself and your ability to mediate? Are there any internal demands, any "shoulds" or "musts" you didn't live up to?

2. In what situation did these thoughts come up? What was it that you did that you responded to and that you would have liked to have done differently?

3. What do you feel when you allow yourself to hear these thoughts? Stop for a moment and really allow these feelings to be felt.

4. What needs are these feelings telling you about? Which needs were not met by the way you behaved during the mediation?

5. Now ask yourself which of your needs you tried to meet by what you did. Take a moment to really let your answers surface and reflect on what you can learn from this that you can use in your next mediation. Also think about what you can do differently next time, things you imagine would better meet the needs you connected with in questions 3 and 4.

Celebrate your successes and learn from them

Use this evaluation after a mediation you feel happy with. This is another way to learn more about mediation, to take some time to reflect on what works, and harvest learning from that.

1. Start by thinking about what you are saying to yourself. Write down any positive judgments you have about yourself.

2. After that, find clear observations on what you did that you are especially happy about.

3. What do you feel when you reflect on this? Stop for a moment and allow yourself to really feel these feelings.

4. What are the needs that these feelings are telling you about? Which of your needs were met by what you did during the mediation? Take a moment to really enjoy the power you have to enrich your own and other peoples' lives.

5. Take a moment to really let your answers sink in and think about what you can learn from this. Is there something you can use as a reminder for the next time you mediate?

A Helping Hand
Mediation with Nonviolent Communication

Chapter 10

Mediation between children

Mediation between children

The principles in this book can be used in mediation between people regardless of age, culture, gender, religious or ethnic background. There are, of course, some differences in what we pay attention to as mediators in various situations. One difference between mediation between adults and mediation between children (at least with young children), can be that a child's vocabulary isn't as large. In this case we can use our creativity to find different ways to mediate and communicate.

In my experience I have found that children, even fairly young children, understand more words than they can express. They will also receive support more often and effectively than adults, leading to an increased flow in the mediation.

How we adults act when children have a conflict affects all relationships in the family, preschool groups, school classes and other situations where adults and children interact. Moreover, it not only affects children in the very moment of conflict, but also in the long run. How we handle conflicts is of great importance and can lead to either an increase or a decrease in security or trust.

There are many ways in which you as an adult can help children who have conflicts. You can, for example, differentiate interpretations from clear observations; translate judgments into what someone is feeling and needing; listen and really try to understand children and also refrain from making comparisons, demands or threats. You will give children a precious gift that will last a lifetime. Your presence can, in addition to helping them manage conflict, also show children that it is possible to do so in a way that can enrich everyone involved.

Adults often try to protect children from emotional and physical pain. We worry that our children will not learn to manage relationships in a peaceful way. Many of us have strong values about the importance of sharing, to ensure that everyone can be part of the community. We want our children to fit in, learn to cooperate and socialize with others.

When a disagreement arises, few of us stop to connect with what we value or with what we wish for our children. Some of us let our children handle the problems themselves, others get involved and try to help the children resolve the conflict. We may, for example, point out that this child had the toy first, and make sure that the child gets it back. Some remind children that "sharing" or "taking turns" is important. Others use some sort of punishment. Even though these things may create temporary peace in a conflict, they often weaken our ability to thoroughly satisfy both our children's and our own needs. This ability is undermined by the fact that we do not create an opportunity to address the conflict in a way that puts attention on everyone's needs.

What can we do if we really would like to use a conflict between children as an opportunity for us all to learn how we can live in peace, to satisfy everyone's needs, to create genuine cooperation and to contribute to genuine compassion? I think we best show what we want children to do by our own behavior. The expression "Children do what we do, not what we say" is very often true. For me it is very important to show children that everyone's needs are important and can be met. To bring out that message, I need to find ways of showing it, rather than just telling it to a child. Raising our voice is hardly the best way to teach children not to raise theirs. If I don't want children to use their physical strength against another child, one way is to not use my own physical advantage to teach them not to beat or kick one another.

I often hear adults say to a child: "Don't touch!", while at the same time they are taking something from the child's hand and giving it to another child. Taking an object from the child may seem quite logical to the adult, who is trying to meet a need for justice, care and support in doing so. However, it may be just as logical to the child to take something that another child is playing with, in order to meet his needs for play, fun and freedom. When we prevent children from doing what they are doing in an attempt to meet their needs, without simultaneosly trying to think how these needs could be met in some other way, we often contribute to an escalation of the conflict.

I could fill an entire book with what we can think about if we want to mediate between children, but I will just give a few examples, which hopefully can serve as a wake-up call, or better yet, serve as inspiration.

If the grownup chooses to listen to both sides

The adult listens to both children's feelings and needs. This can take a short time or a long time, depending on how familiar the children are with receiving support and how upset they are. In the situation with the car, the girl probably wants to feel confident that she will be able to play with the car later. The boy's needs might be to have fun and be free to play the way he likes.

A Helping Hand
Mediation with Nonviolent Communication

It may take a while for both to be heard, but then try to find a way to move forward together, meeting both children's needs. The adult does not take over the conflict, nor doeas the adult disregard how the children solve it.

If the adult chooses side

A Helping Hand
Mediation with Nonviolent Communication

A Helping Hand
Mediation with Nonviolent Communication

If the grownup chooses the other side

A Helping Hand
Mediation with Nonviolent Communication

If parents (or others adults) choose sides in children's conflicts, they often escalate, because the core issue in the conflict is not dealt with. One child might be satisfied, at least for a while, but now the other child is also in conflict with the parent. Also, parents miss a valuable opportunity to show children how it is possible to act in other ways than having one win and one lose.

Many of us would never dream of openly judging or labeling adults in the way we often do with children. We might for example say a child is "stupid" or "egoistic". At the same time we expect children to show us respect and care for us, in a situation where it can be difficult for them to experience respect and care for themselves.

If the adult chooses not to intervene

Most children have learned early on to compete. Therefore, conflicts (both children's and adult's) are often handled by the principle "the strongest wins". If a child asks an adult to help deal with a conflict and hears: "You can handle this yourselves", we miss a chance to show that it is possible to take everyone's needs into account, even in a conflict. We have also indirectly supported a culture based on competition or the ability to assert yourself.

In my NVC work, parents have often shared their disappointing experiences of trying to mediate between their children. They have tried, but later experienced that the conflict worsened. This has led them to not try at all. At a later stage, many have realized that they have tried to mediate by comparing and arguing about what is "right" or "fair". Many have also discovered what a difference it makes to mediate with a focus on meeting both parties' rather than just on one or the other.

Children often find ways to manage conflicts without the support of adults. At the same time, they can feel quite lonely and insecure if the adult they ask for help tells them to deal with the conflict themselves. I wish more people would respond to conflicts as something that affects us all and see that conflicts can provide us with unique opportunities for learning and cooperation.

If the adult stops the conflict rather than attempting to mediate

If the parent (or other adult) is asked to help out in a conflict and threatens a punishment or in any other way tries to stop the conflict, several things can happen. First, the adult misses an opportunity to teach children something about conflicts. It is easy for children to perceive conflict as something that is taboo; that conflicts are something preferably to be avoided or hidden. Here, parents could instead clarify that conflicts are natural and that they can be managed. Children could also learn how valuable it can be to get help from a third party, one who doesn't take sides in the midst of a challenging situation.

When conflicts are covered up, or when the one who has the most power (usually the parent or adult) tries to ban them, they often grow and become increasingly more difficult to manage each time they occur. When a parent raises his voice or even yells at children to stop fighting, the parent does not demonstrate a new way of managing conflict.

The parent rather reinforces the idea that screaming and threatening are effective ways to manage conflicts, at least if you are bigger or have more power.

If the adult compares

I have often heard adults use comparisons in an attempt to help children deal with conflicts. Although the intention is to help, it can, if it happens often, have tragic consequences. It frequently leads to more conflicts, creates more distance within the family and, maybe worst of all, contributes to low self-esteem in children. It is easy to use comparisons when we get angry and say things like "Why can't you ever be on time like your siblings?" To compare in a "positive" way can also be unconstructive: "Great, you made it even quicker than your brother!"

We may say this impulsively when we suddenly are surprised and thrilled. In both cases there are judgments being made and so it is

Why can't you be more like your sister? She is always so generous.

more constructive for everyone involved if you as the adult describe what you see or hear rather than compare.

In the pictures on the previous page, the adult shows that he thinks it is important to give and to be generous. However, it is too easy to hear that as a person, we "should" be generous, not because we have a genuine wish to give to others, but because it is right to do so, or because we want to be loved.

Most adults value honesty and authenticity, and yet this is probably is not what we are laying the grounds for through this kind of action. Here, the adult contributes to creating competition, rather than connection between the children. In the long run this can lead to difficulties in cooperating and to conflicts that are more difficult to handle in the future.

More results of comparing

Describe what you see rather than compare

> I see that you're both pulling the kite – do you need my help?

Here the adult catches the children's attention and makes a connection. He can now try to help them deal with the situation. When we stick with observations, what we see rather than judging what someone is or what they ought to do differently, it is easier for both parties to have faith that you can help them. This is as true for children as it is for adults.

The next step is to understand what it is both children need and to support them in finding other ways to meet everyone's needs.

Using power to protect

Sometimes we might not succeed in mediating between children and so the conflict escalates. We could worry that someone might get hurt. Then we may perhaps use our physical advantage to prevent this from happening. In order to maintain a good relationship, it is important that we intervene with the intention to protect and not to punish.

After having used the power we have to protect someone from getting hurt, it is important to go back as soon as possible to have a dialogue with the intention of creating connection and mutual respect. If we protect a child

To use power to punish

To use power to protect

from physical pain, it can contribute to an improved security for everyone, but only if we do it while maintaining respect for everyone involved.

After we have intervened, and children have calmed down enough so that no one is hurt, we can help them to create a connection with each other. Once they have understood each other and want to try to find solutions that can work for everyone, they will often find solutions themselves. Here is an example of the value of intervening to protect, rather than to punish.

One of my friends is a single parent who struggles financially at times. Every unforeseen expense is a challenge. When her son brought a ball indoors to play, she asked him to stop playing with the ball inside, as the ball could hit and break something. Still he continued, and when she asked me for advice, I suggested that she could tell him what she wanted him to do, and why, rather than talk about what she didn't want him to do.

She tried asking him to roll the ball on the floor and explained that it was because she didn't want anything to break. He continued to bounce the ball. After having heard her try to approach him with empathy a couple of times, and also having asked him to roll the ball still with no success, I suggested that she instead could take the ball away from him to protect their shared resources.

"But I want him to feel free," she replied tiredly. I waited and watched as she several times asked him to stop bouncing the ball. She got more and more irritated. In the end she got fed up, violently took away the ball from her son and firmly hid it away. He was of course very disappointed and expressed this out loud. At this point the mother herself was irritated (because she had waited so long to stand up for her needs), so it was difficult for her to respond to what he felt with empathy and support.

We talked about this a couple days later and she realized that she had wanted to stand up for her own need for security and take away the ball sooner. She realized that she probably would have been much more able to respond to her son's disappointment with understanding and tenderness if she hadn't waited to act until she got angry.

If an adult is angry and punishes a child for something he or she has done, it will probably be difficult to recreate the connection on the spot. When we are angry, our heads are so full of judgments that we rarely can be open to another person's (regardless of size) feelings and needs. We are likely to need some time to get in touch with ourselves and our own needs again. It can also take some time for the child to rebuild respect and trust in relation to the adult who has for example called the child "mean". Other children in the room may also become frightened and have difficulties in feeling safe enough to open up to an adult whom they have seen get angry.

When an adult tries to mediate by using punishment

One day at the beach my son Neo saw a boy and a girl playing. He had played with the boy, Tom, before, and ran towards them to join their play. Tom, who speaks another language than Neo, shouted something at him and threw sand in his face.

Neo came crying and flung himself into my arms asking why the boy did that. At the same time Tom's father, who had seen it all, slapped Tom in the face and yelled at him.

As I don't speak their language, I can only guess it was something like "that is no way to behave! " or "that was a stupid thing to do! "

The boy started crying. Everything happened so fast that Neo, lying in my arms, didn't see anything other than Tom starting to cry. Neo looked up and asked, "why is Tom crying?

"I guess it is because it hurts that his daddy hit him" I answered.

"Why did he hit him?" Neo asked and started crying even more.

The boy's mother said to Neo (in halting English, so I understood the words): "Everything is alright now, look Tom is crying, so now you can forgive him!"

I guess this was Tom's parent's way to help repair the broken connection between the boys.

My guess is that these parents have been "marinated" in the same mind-set as so many of us. They have probably learned like the majority of people around the globe, that the one who has done 'wrong' must be punished. When the person has been punished and made to suffer, the crime is atoned for and can be forgiven. I doubt that Tom learned what his parents wanted him to learn from this. It was probably most confusing and

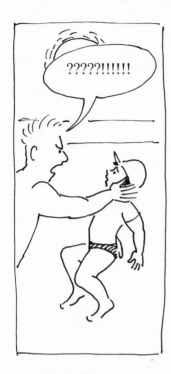

painful for him, as it was for Neo. And it was a long time after this incident before they played together again.

A Helping Hand
Mediation with Nonviolent Communication

Mediate between children

My experience of mediating between children is that it is both easier and harder than to mediate between adults. Harder because it challenges the static ideas most of us have about how a child is or should be.

On the other hand, it may be easier because children are often more direct and show more clearly what they feel.

This exercise can be used both as the basis for role-play in a group and as a writing exercise. Think of a situation when you were not satisfied with how you tried to help two children connect. It can be between one of your own children and one of their friends, between two of your children or between two other children.

1. Describe the situation briefly. Use observations to create clarity within yourself.

2. What do you feel when you think about this situation?

3. Which of your needs would you have liked to have met in this situation?

4. Are there any requests you would like to express to yourself or to the children now or in the past?

5. Think of one of the children and write down what you guess this child was feeling and needing.

Then think about what could be said to the child if you want to convey empathy for her/his feelings and needs. Write down how you think that the child would respond.

6. Think of the second child and write down what you think that child knows and needs.

7. Then write down what you could express to this child if you want to convey empathy for this child's feelings and needs.

8. Write down how you think the child would respond.

9. Then write down an answer to each child's expressions. Make empathy guesses about what might be going on in them. Also write down how you could express your own feelings, needs and requests.

Continue the dialogue as long as it feels meaningful, or until you can find a solution that could meet both children's needs.

Some final words

Some final words

For me, to act as third party is like dancing a dance where I can try to control my dance partner, but where the movements and steps are never predetermined. It is up to me to make sure that we do not collide and to be attentive about how the other person is experiencing the dance. A mediation process is never predictable, and I never cease to be amazed at what can happen when people are supported in connecting with each other. I have great reverence for being able to take part in mediations whenever they take place.

Everyone can learn to mediate. I deeply believe this to be true. Your view of human nature determines whether it will be easy or difficult. If you have learned that people can be divided into good and evil, it will probably be a challenge to listen and really hear what is deeply human in some people. However, if you have learned that people have dreams, values and needs as a driving force behind everything they do, it will be a bit easier. With the help of this book, I hope to have inspired you to explore a view of human nature that is based on the idea that everything people do, comes from attempting to meet needs. Now is your chance to use these tools in helping people to meet.

Most of us need training to be able to mediate in an effective way. I hope that this book, and especially the exercises, can provide you with some of that training. A sound theoretical background does not exclude the need to practise, practise, practise. In order to really understand how you can contribute as a third party, you need to stick your neck out and dare to do it "for real". After you have tried your hand at mediating, either formally or informally, it can be useful to re-read this book. A repetition of the theoretical grounds, especially after having actively practiced them, can be of great help to move forward and learn even more.

There are also trainings you can attend in order to learn together with others. See, www.friareliv.se/eng for suggestions.

Good luck!

Study plan

This study plan is intended for a group meeting six times or more, 2-3 hours each time. The exercises are best suited for groups of 3 to 12 people. Find a location that is sufficiently private to be able to do role plays without having to worry that others might be disturbed.

The more prepared everyone is when coming to each session, the more you can learn. Therefore, encourage one another to study the agreed upon text sections before each session and do the suggested exercises.

First session

Preparation: Read chapters 1-2 and 5 before you meet.
Also read through the text "Be clear about your purpose in mediating" in Chapter 7 on page 119 as preparation for doing the exercise together.
Let everyone briefly share what makes them want to participate in this group. Discuss the first chapters that you have read, and take a moment to share your understanding of the purpose of mediation.
Do the exercise "Be clear about your purpose in mediating" in Chapter 7 on page 119 (best if everyone has done part of the exercise the session) and share how this was for you. Support each other in finding one's purpose in mediating, as well as any pitfalls, opportunities and growth areas.

Second session

Preparation: Read Chapter 6, as well as the exercises in Chapter 7.
Talk about your understanding of the different tools of "the hand".
Do the exercise "Observation or interpretation, depending on the point of view" in Chapter 5 on page 77
Do the exercise "Exercise to translate what is being said so that it creates connection" in Chapter 7 on page 124

Third session

Preparation: Read Chapters 3 and 4. Review any text on self-empathy and "how to interrupt" in Chapter 6 on page 96. Share your thoughts on passivity. What feelings, dreams, requests or inner demands does Chapter 3 awaken?

Do "An exercise in pulling someone by the ear" in Chapter 7 on page 129. Also do the exercises about "interrupting" and giving first aid-empathy in Chapter 7 on page 134.

Fourth session

Preparation: Read Chapter 8 and do the exercise in Chapter 3 about how you can deal with a situation when people around you are in a conflict. In the session, you can share your discoveries from this exercise.

Do "Exercise informal mediation - in slow motion" on page 154 in Chapter 7. You might want to do it in writing and in the form of a role play where you can use all of your previous knowledge. You can go deeper into a particular role play or choose to try a variety of situations.

Fifth session

Preparation: Read Chapter 9.

Do the exercise "Practicing formal mediation - in slow motion" from Chapter 8 from page 180.

Practice what the mediator can say at the beginning of a mediation and evaluate together what really needs to be said, what provides security and so on. Take inspiration from the suggestions in Chapter 9.

Sixth session and onwards

Preparation: Read Chapter 10. Review any of the previous mediation exercises if you want to practice specific skills, or practice mediating in the form of a role play.

Everyday expression for needs

Sometimes people get stuck on particular words and phrases, and this can complicate the mediation. If I as a mediator notice this, it can be helpful to have access to several different ways of expressing the same thing. Be creative. Find out what works in each situation.

The phrases below are suggestions for how you can expand your repertoire to express needs, without always using the word "need". On the dotted line, you can insert any word that describes a need.

These phrases can be used as long as your attention is on needs or values, and when you remind yourself that these are not bound to a person, place, time or specific action. If you aren't clear whether or not you want to listen for or express needs, you risk blurring the distinction between needs and strategies to meet needs.

Since you need ...

Because you long for ...

Because you want ...

Since you believe ...

Because you remember ...

Because you love ...

Since you are interested in ...

Because you enjoy...

Because you like ...

Since you value ...

Since you prefer ...

A Helping Hand
Mediation with Nonviolent Communication

Because you hope ...

Because it's important for you to have ...

Because you look forward to ...

Because what you get energy from is ...

Since something you live for is ...

... is fun for you

... is important / is important to you

... makes your life more meaningful

... helps you feel good

... helps you feel happy

Clearly expressing how <u>I am</u> without blaming or criticizing

Empathically receiving how <u>you are</u> without hearing blame or criticism

Observations

What I observe (see, hear, remember, imagine, free from my evaluations) that does or does not contribute to my well-being:

What you observe (see, hear, remember, imagine, free from your evaluations) that does or does not contribute to your well-being:

"When I (see, hear)..."

"When you see/hear..."
(Sometimes unspoken when offering empathy)

Feeling

How I feel (emotion or sensation rather than thought) in relation to what I observe:

How you feel (emotion or sensation rather than thought) in relation to what you observe:

"I feel ..."

"You feel...?"

Need

What I need or value (rather than a preference, or a specific action) that causes my feelings:
" . . . because I need/value . . . "

What you need or value (rather than a preference, or a specific action) that causes your feelings:

"because you need/value...?"

"Because I need/value..."

Request

The concrete actions I would like taken:

The concrete actions you would like taken:

"Would you be willing to ...?"

"Would you like ...?"
(Sometimes unspoken when offering empathy)

Some basic feelings we all have

Feelings when needs are fulfilled

Amazed	Fulfilled	Joyous	Stimulated
Comfortable	Glad	Moved	Surprised
Confident	Hopeful	Optimistic	Thankful
Eager	Inspired	Proud	Touched
Energetic	Intrigued	Relieved	Trustful

Feelings when needs are not fullfilled

Angry	Discouraged	Hopeless	Overwhelmed
Annoyed	Distressed	Impatient	Puzzled
Concerned	Embarrassed	Irritated	Reluctant
Confused	Frustrated	Lonely	Sad
Disappointed	Helpless	Nervous	Uncomfortable

Some basic needs we all have

Autonomy
- Choosing dreams/goals/values
- Choosing plans for fulfilling one's dreams, goals, values

Celebration
- Celebrating the creation of life and dreams fulfilled
- Celebrating losses: loved ones, dreams, etc. (mourning)

Integrity
- Authenticity • Creativity
- Meaning • Self-worth

Interdependence
- Acceptance • Appreciation
- Closeness • Community
- Consideration
- Contribution to the enrichment of life
- Emotional Safety • Empathy

Physical Nurturance
- Air • Food
- Movement, exercise
- Protection from life-threatening forms of life: viruses, bacteria, insects, predatory animals
- Rest • Sexual expression
- Shelter • Touch • Water

Play
- Fun • Laughter

Spiritual Communion
- Beauty • Harmony
- Inspiration • Order • Peace
- Honesty (the empowering honesty that enables us to learn from our limitations)
- Love • Reassurance
- Respect • Support
- Trust • Understanding

References and literature

Böhm & Kaplan (2006), Hämnd och att avstå från att ge igen. Natur och Kultur.

Dass (1998) How Can I Help? - Stories and Reflections on Service.

Diamond, Jared (1999) Guns, Germs, and Steel: The Fates of Human Societies W. W. Norton & Company.

Clark, E Mary (2002), In search of human nature. Routledge.

Eisler, Riane (1998), The Chalice and the Blade: Our History, Our Future. Harper.

Eisler, Riane (1996), Sacred Pleasure: Sex, Myth, and the Politics of the Body. Harper.

Eisler, Riane (2007) The Real Wealth of Nations: Creating a Caring Economics. Berrett-Koehler

Frankl, Viktor (2006) Man's Search for Meaning -meaning. Beacon Press.

Hartmann, Thom. (2001) The Last Hours of Ancient Sunlight. Hodder and Stoughton.

Fisher & Ury (1987), Getting to Yes. Arrow Books Limited.

Jordan, Thomas (2007), Att hantera och förebygga konflikter på arbetsplatsen. Lärarförbundet.

Kashtan, Inbal (2004),Parenting From Your Heart - Sharing the Gifts of Compassion, Connection and Choice. Puddle Dancer Press.

Larsson, Liv (2004), Nonviolent Communication i praktiken: arbetsbok för att lära sig Nonviolent Communication individuellt eller i grupp. Friare Liv Konsult.

MacKenzie, Mary (2005), Peaceful living Daily Meditations for Living with Love, Healing, and Compassion. Puddle Dancer Press.

Martin, Luther King, Jr (2002), I've Been to the Mountaintop: From a Call to Conscience. Grand Central Publishing.

Marklund, Linda (2007), Skolmedling i teori och praktik. Uppsala universitet.

Milgram, Stanley (2009), Obedience To Authority - An Experimental View. Harpercollins Publishers Inc

Rosenberg, Marshall (2007), Nonviolent Communication, a Language for Life. Puddle Dancer Press

Rosenberg, Marshall (2008), We can work it out. Puddle Dancer Press

Rosenberg, Marshall (2005), Speak Peace In A World Of Conflict, What You Say Next Will Change Your World. Puddle Dancer Press.

Wennstam, Katarina (2005), En riktig våldtäktsman: en bok om samhällets syn på våldtäkt. Albert Bonniers Förlag.

Wink, Walter (2000), Powers that be. Theology for a New Millennium. Doubleday Image.

Wink, Walter (1992), Engaging the Powers Discernment and Resistance in a World of Domination. Fortress P.

Zehr, Howard (2002), The Little Book of Restorative Justice, Good Books.

Åström & Landberg (2004), Peace, love and understanding - blir det effekten av medling vid ungdomsbrottslighet? Umeå universitet.

Electronic sources

www.friareliv.se
www.cnvc.org
www.fnvc.se
www.nonviolentcommunication.com
www.restorativejustice.org
w www.s-f-m.se
www.medlingvidbrott.se
www.bra.se
www.ne.se
www.krf.se
http://sv.wikipedia.org/wiki/Lawrence_Kohlberg

Thank you

I am grateful to finally be able to see this book appearing in English. Since being published in Swedish, the book has been translated into Polish and German, and now into English. Parts of the book have been translated into Thai and used in many mediation trainings in Thailand, to help resolve the longstanding conflict there.

It has been an exciting time since the first edition of the book, as I have learned more about mediation than I ever could have imagined. I clearly see that it is a lifelong process with much to learn about helping people connect. I am grateful for the opportunity to learn and to share my knowledge and experience in so many different places. I am thankful for all the help I have received in order to make this book available in English.

I thank the founder of Nonviolent Communication (NVC), Marshall Rosenberg, for the time and effort he has put into creating and spreading the principles of NVC. I also thank Kay Rung, who has been by my side for a long time. He has given me moral and professional support for more than a decade. We have tried out the exercises in trainings together, as well as tested our skills in NVC in both our private lives and tough situations with other people. Kay is also responsible for the layout and some of the illustrations for this book.

I want to thank my sister Maria Tison-Larsson as well, who has done the illustrations in chapter 10 and has re-edited them every time I have made any comments, though difficult at times. I am also grateful to Johan Rinman who translated this book into English, making it possible for the book to reach more people. I would also like to thank Holly Rinman and Belinda Poropudas for proofreading and re-working much of the text in the English edition.

Lastly, I want to express my appreciation to all the people who have provided suggestions, called attention to errors and pointed out my typos and strange wording. And to those of you who have helped me to overcome my fear about "sticking my neck out" in writing this book. All this support has contributed to the creation of this book and hopefully will help more people find ways to connect beyond their differences.

About the author

Liv Larsson is a Certified Trainer of Nonviolent Communication (NVC) and was trained by Marshall Rosenberg, the founder of NVC. Liv mediates in schools, families and organizations, and teaches mediation and conflict resolution in various contexts. She has written eight books on communication for adults and children.

Liv has translated several of Marshall Rosenberg's books into Swedish. These books have been published by Friare Liv Konsult, which she founded in 1992. Liv has lead workshops since 1990. From 1999 to the present, she has taught NVC in Sweden, Europe and other parts of the world to a wide range of groups such as managers, peace workers, orphanage staff, mediators, theater groups, doctors, teachers and many more. In the past few years she has also specialized in trainings based on "anger, shame and guilt."

She has a passion for in-depth training programs as a way to truly understand systems based on domination and to provide tools to create more life-serving systems in and all around us.

"NVC provides an opportunity to work with the development of individuals, groups and leaders, and therefore contributes not only to individuals, but also to the creation of systems that can help groups of people. I have great confidence in NVC as an approach to create lasting change when we strive to take everyone's needs into account. I see, empathic listening and respectful honesty is a prerequisite for democracy."

Liv Larsson

Email Liv Larsson at liv@friareliv.se